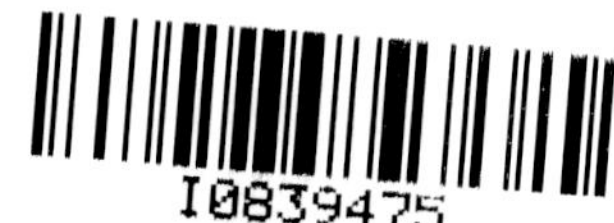

This Book

Belongs to:-

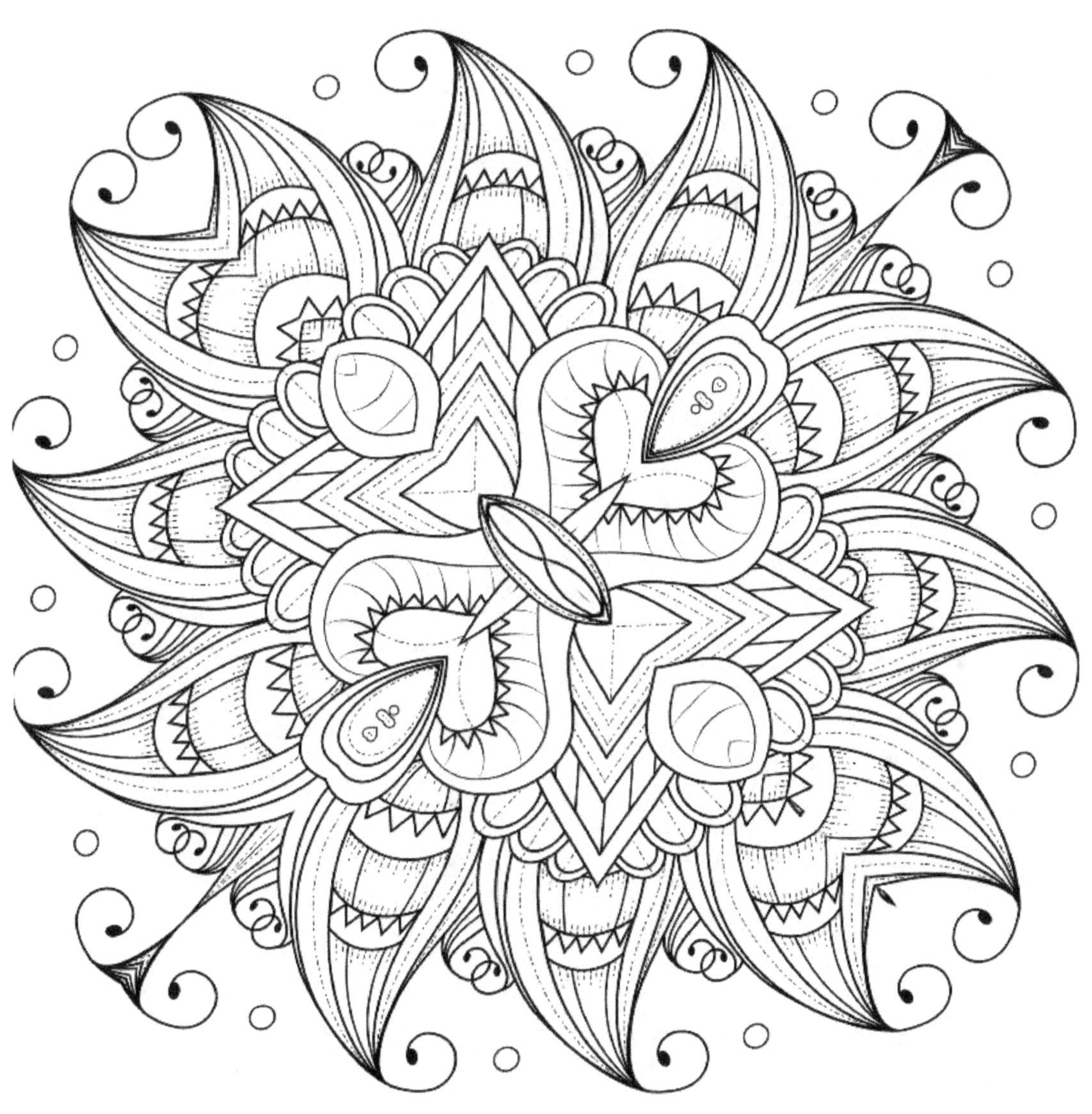

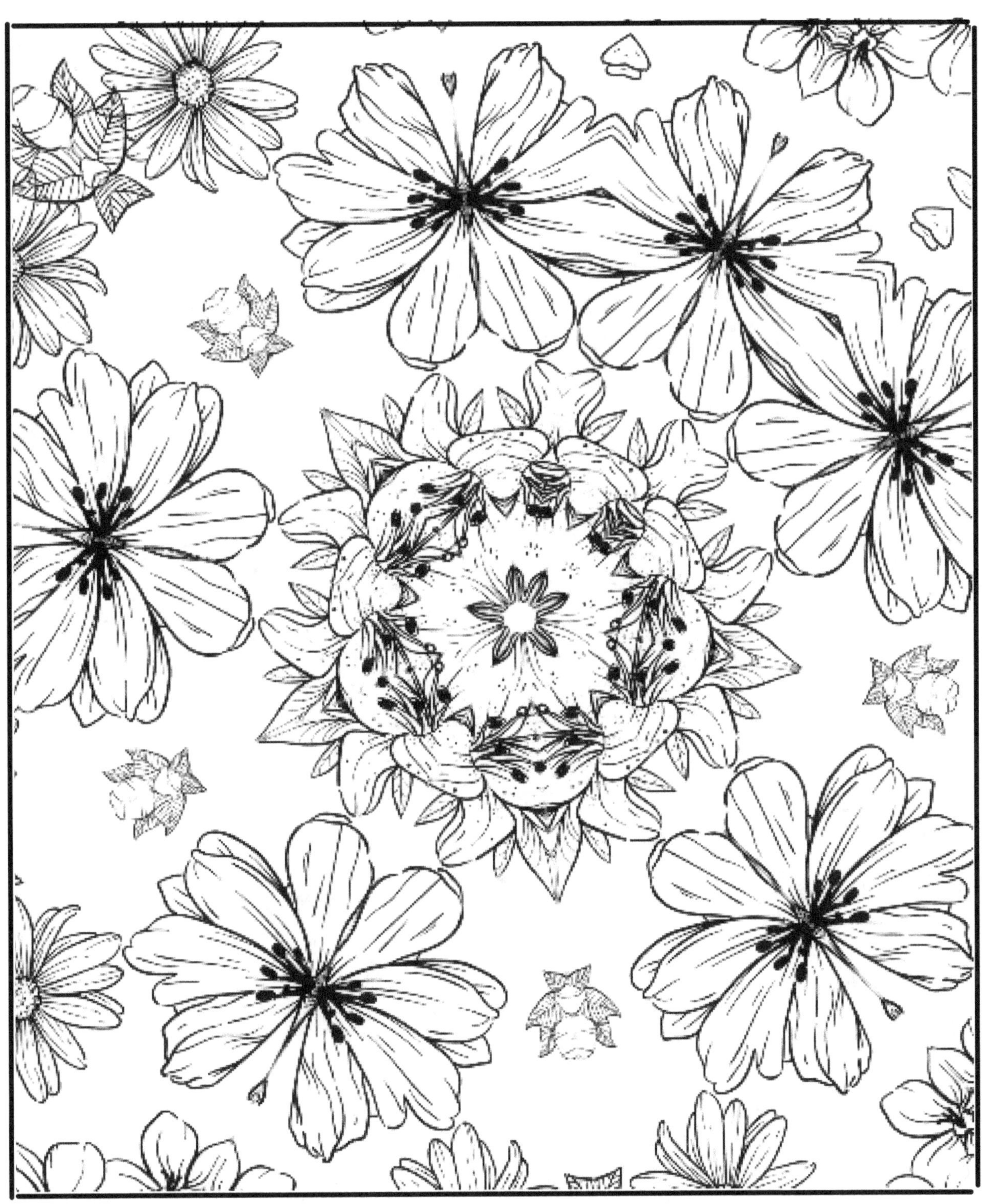

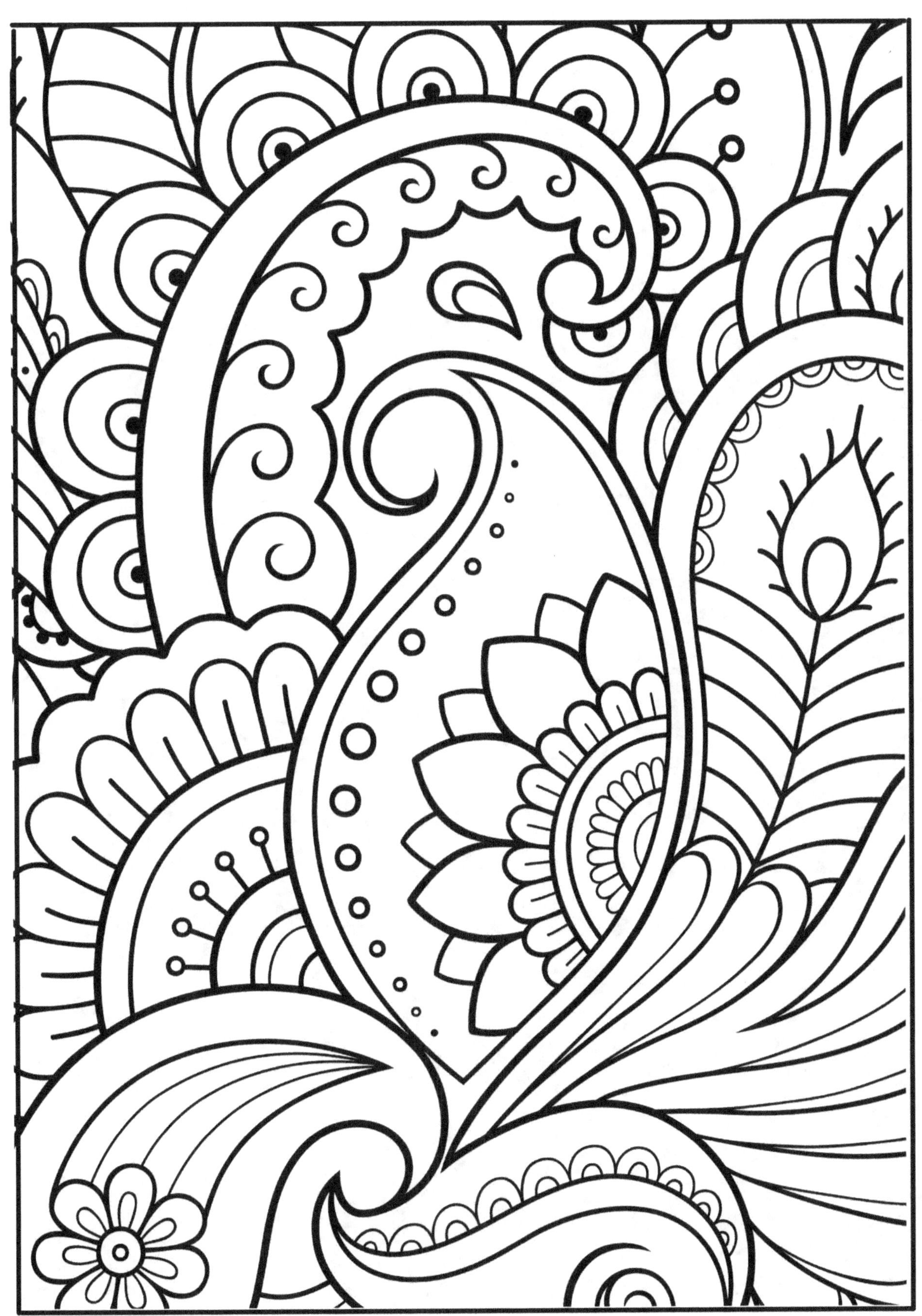

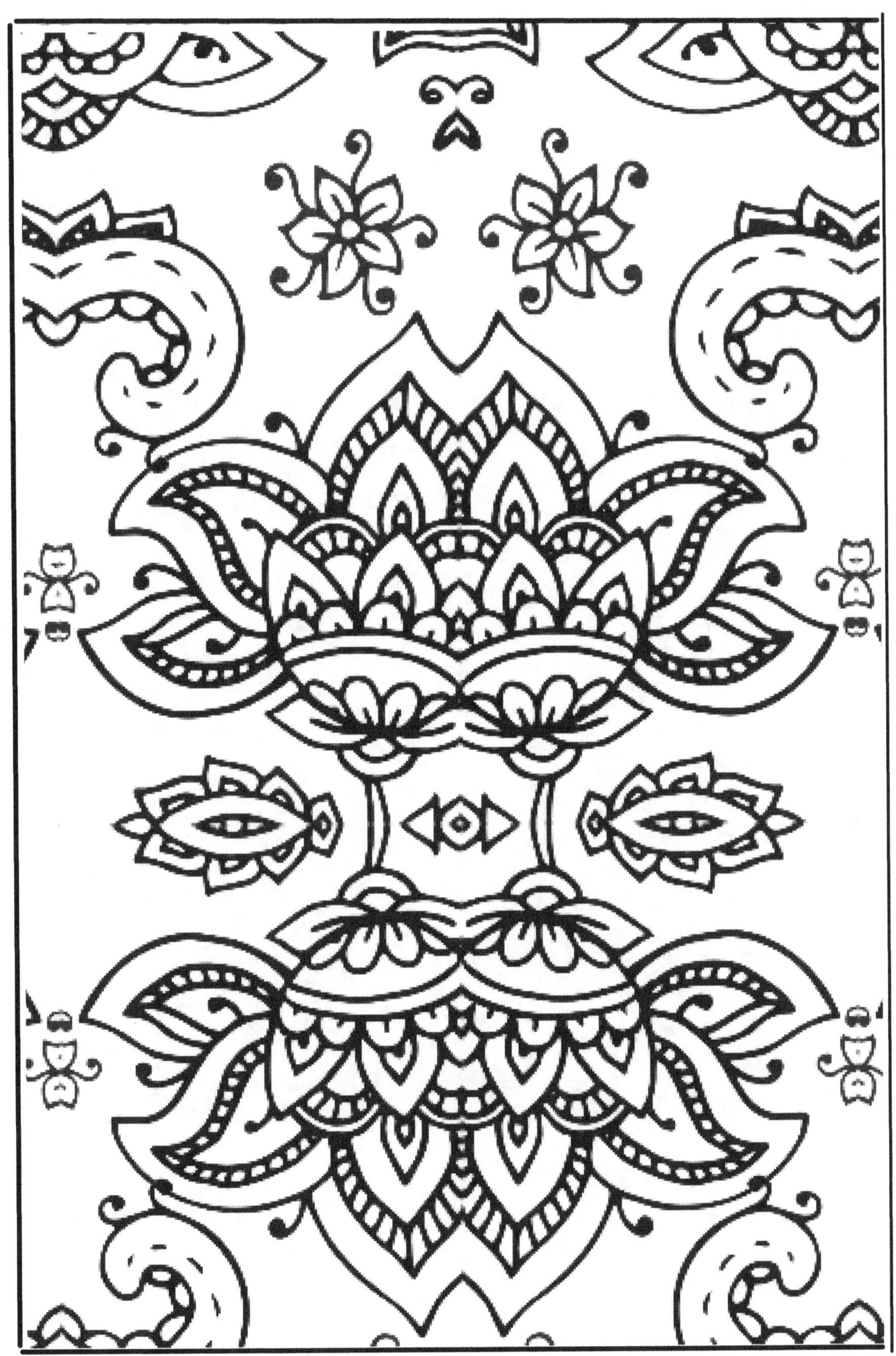

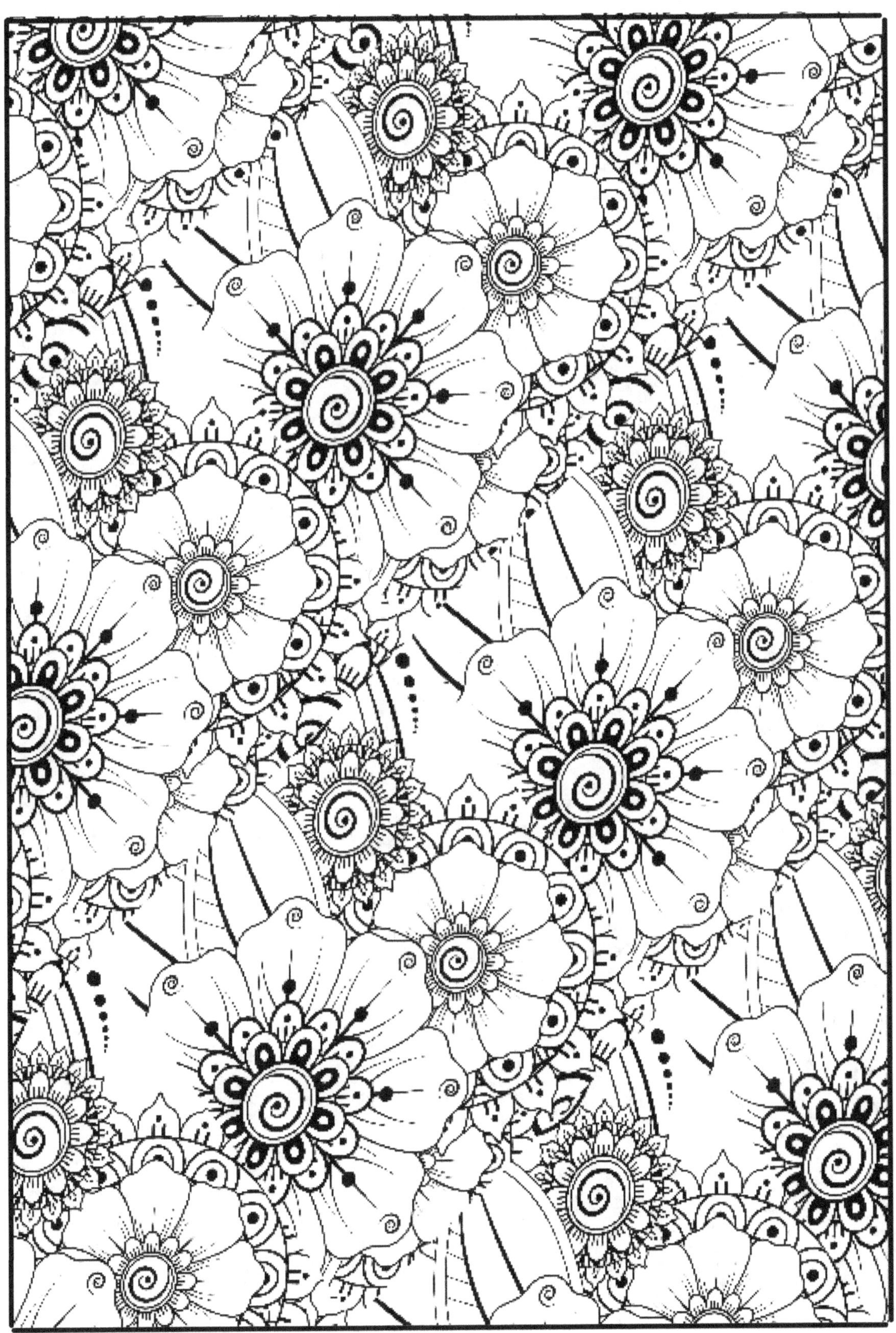

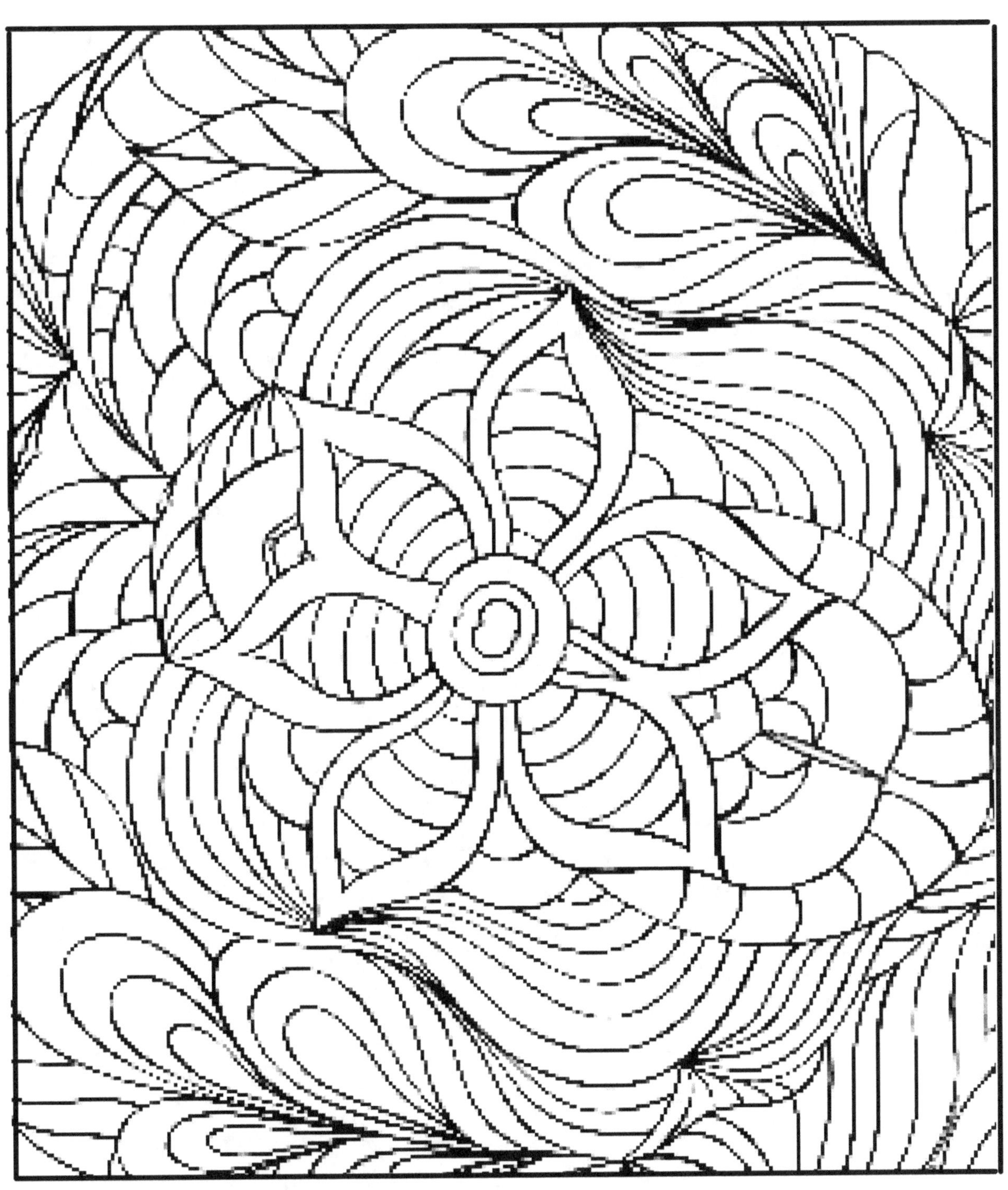

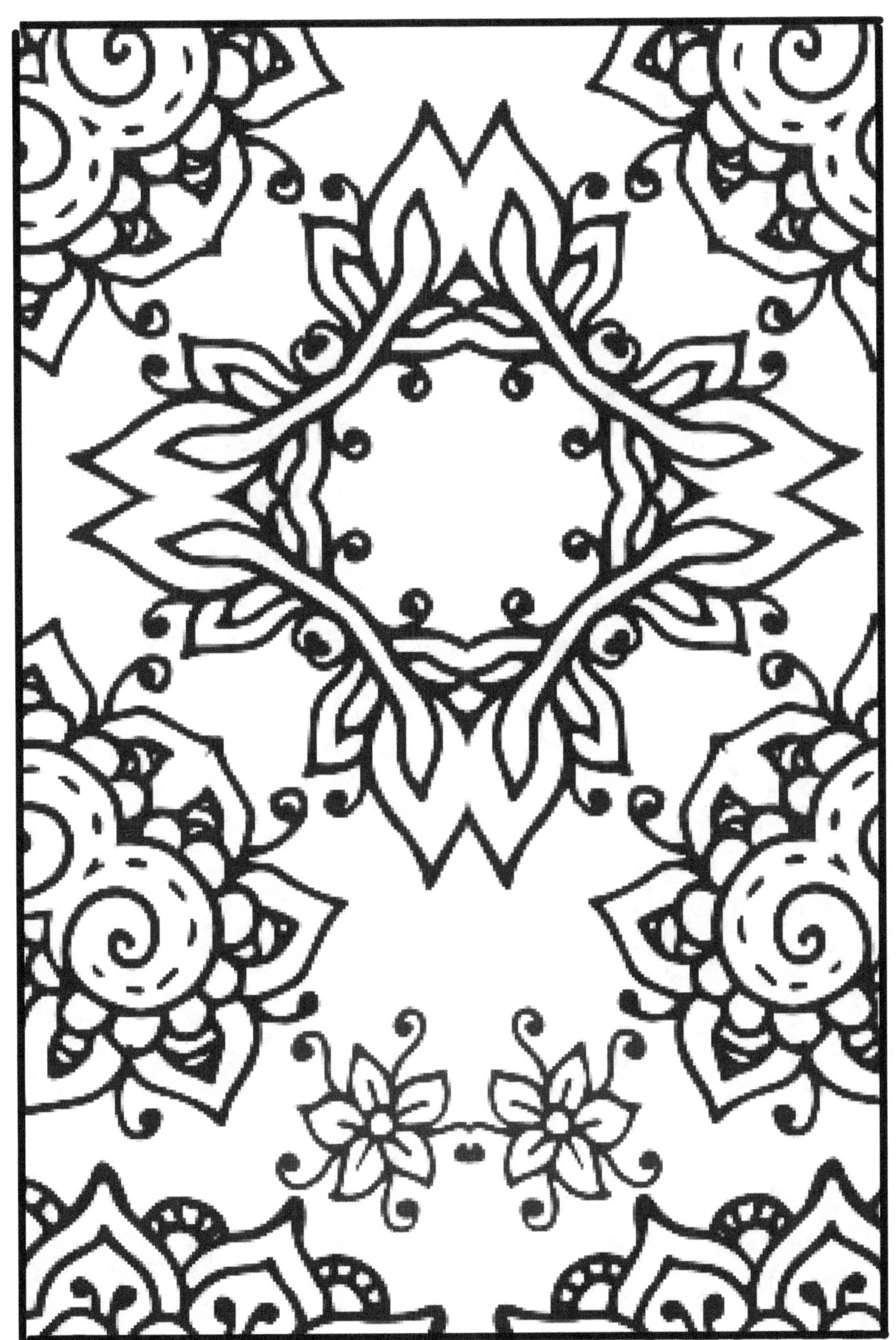

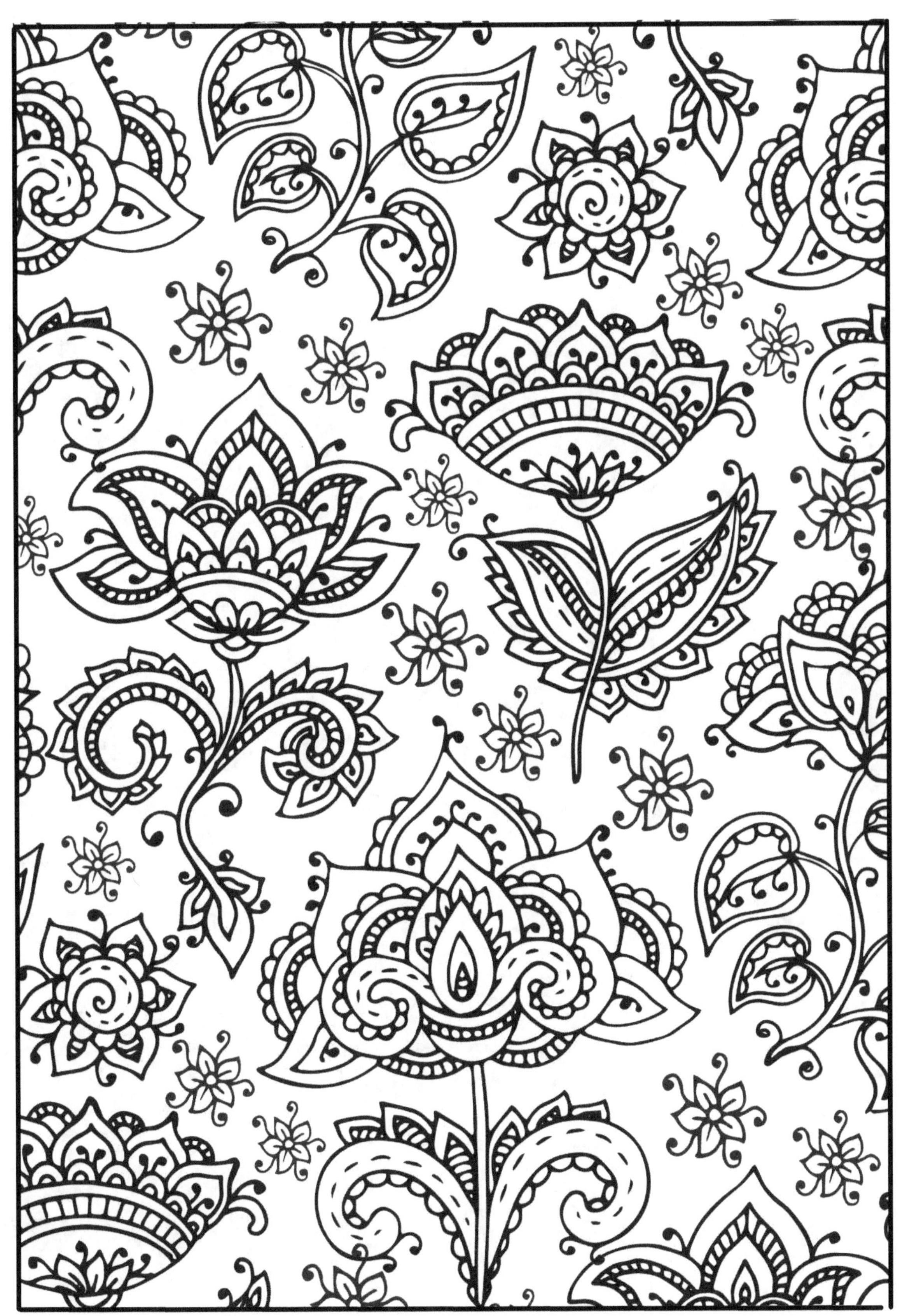

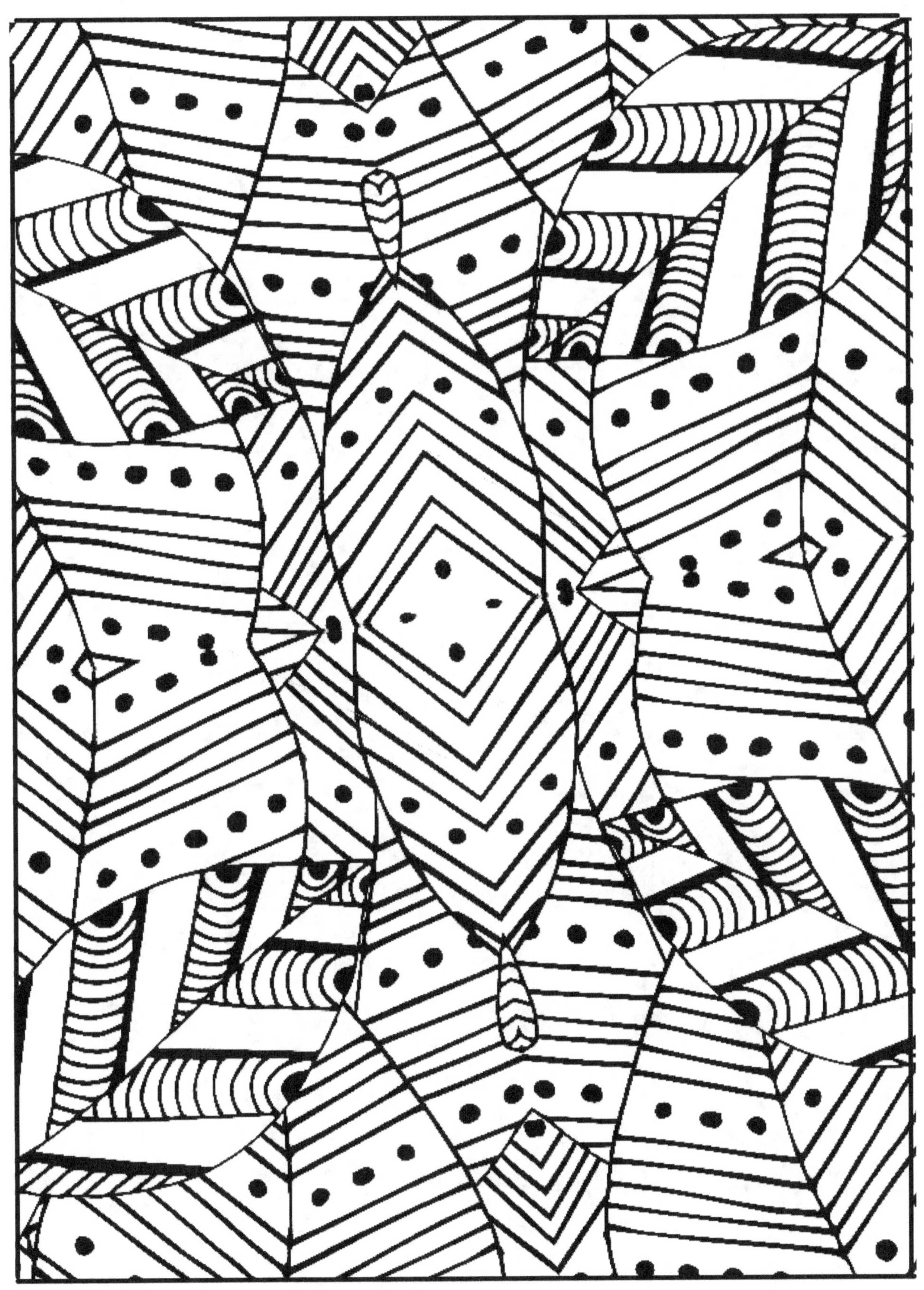

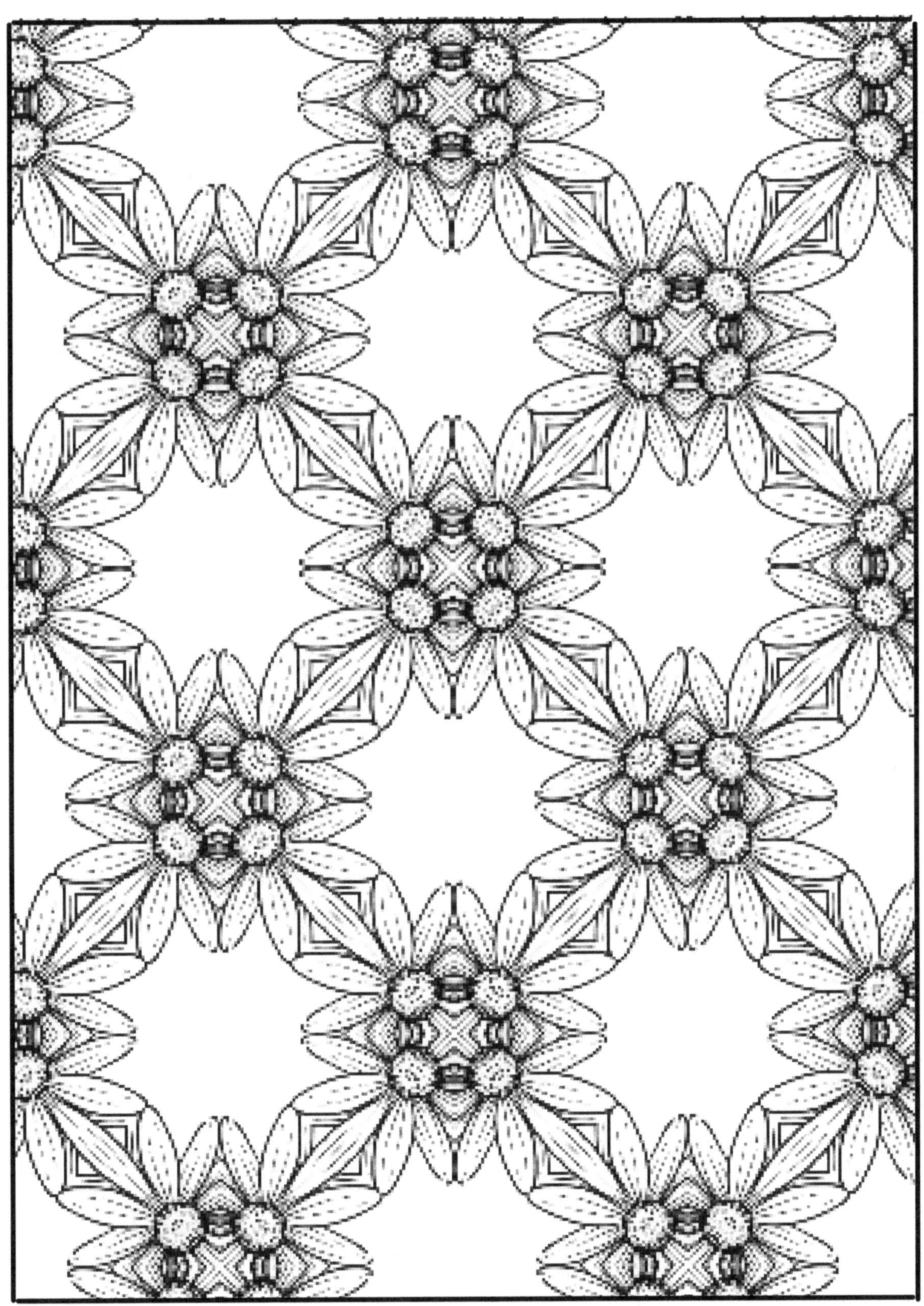

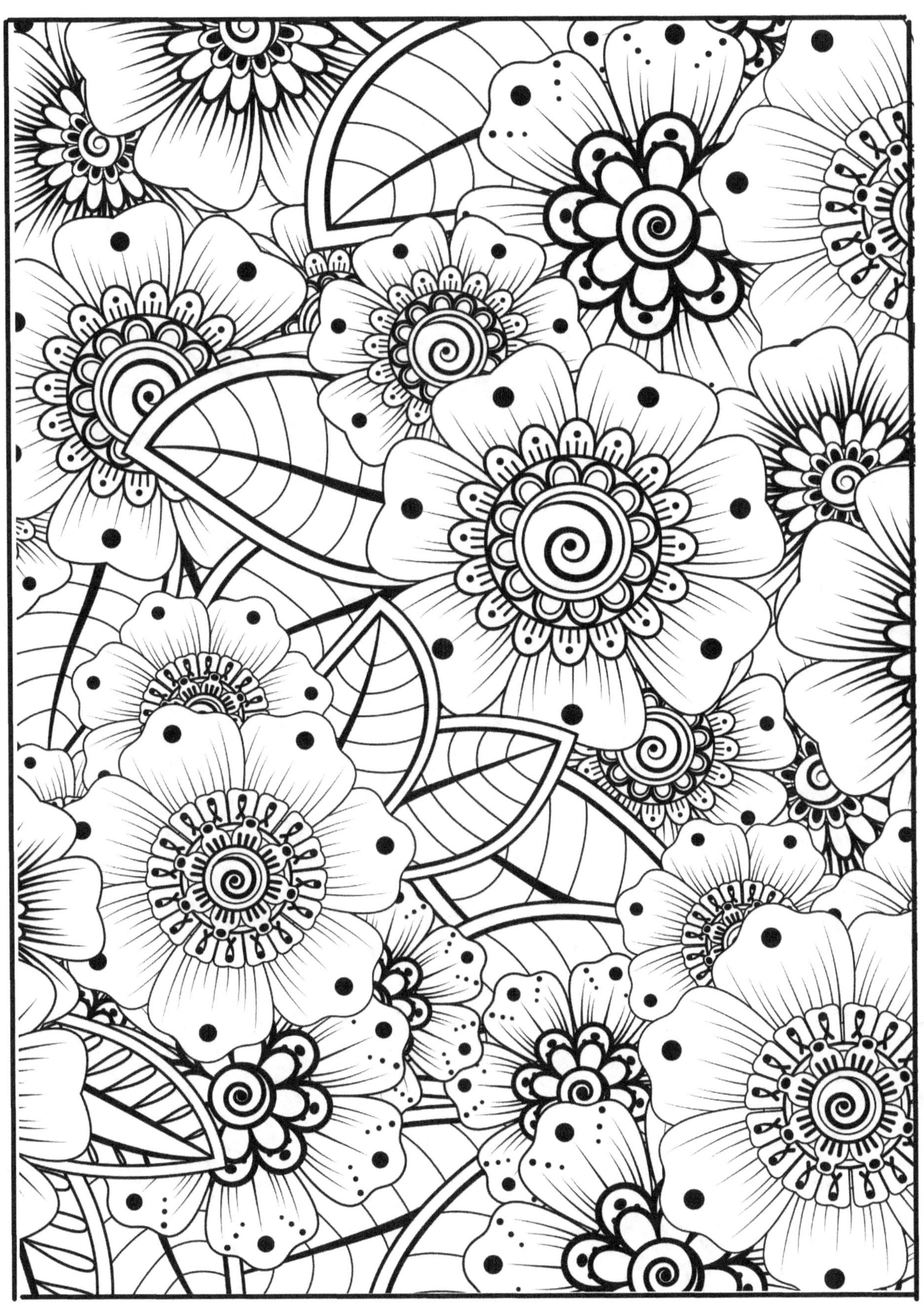

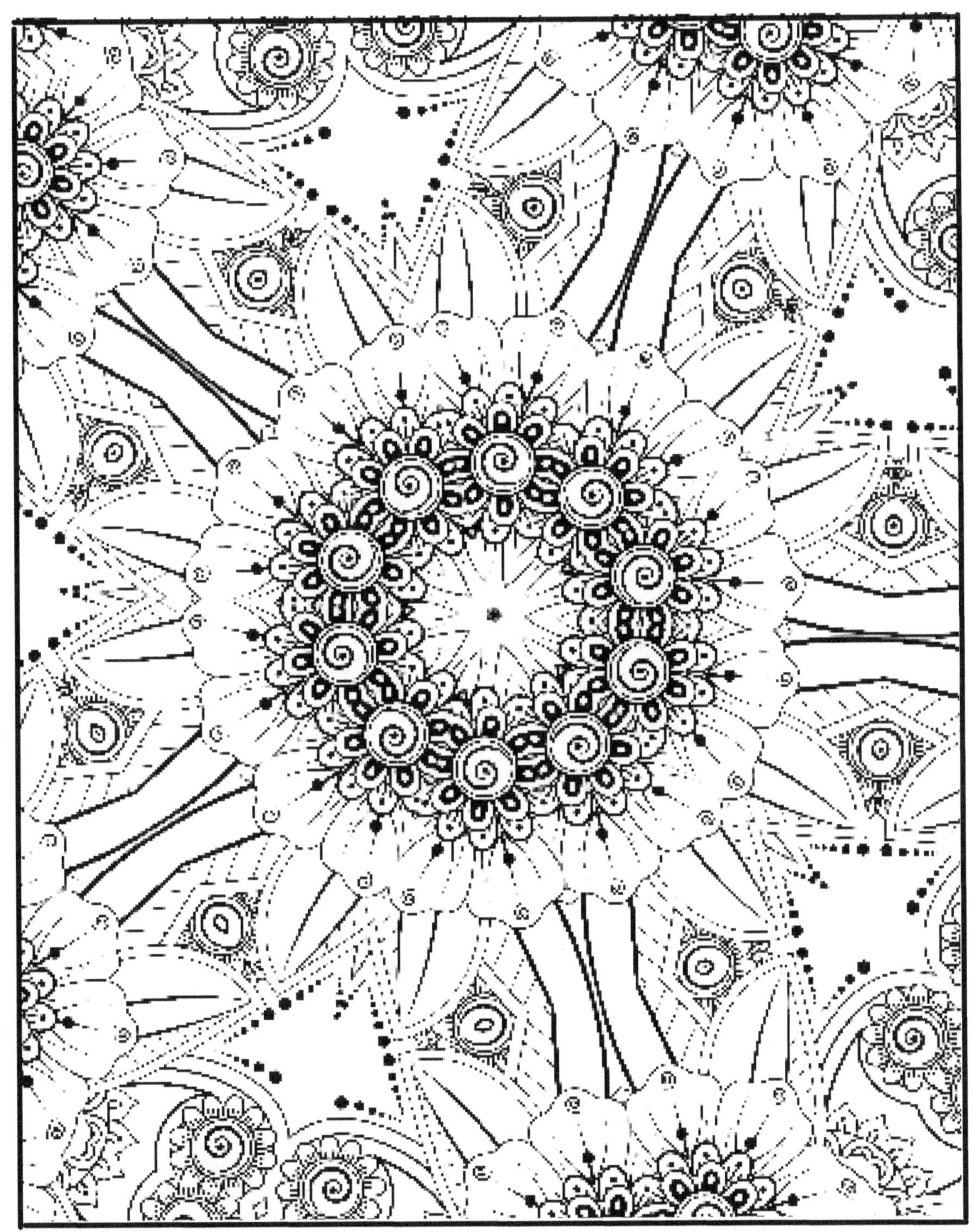

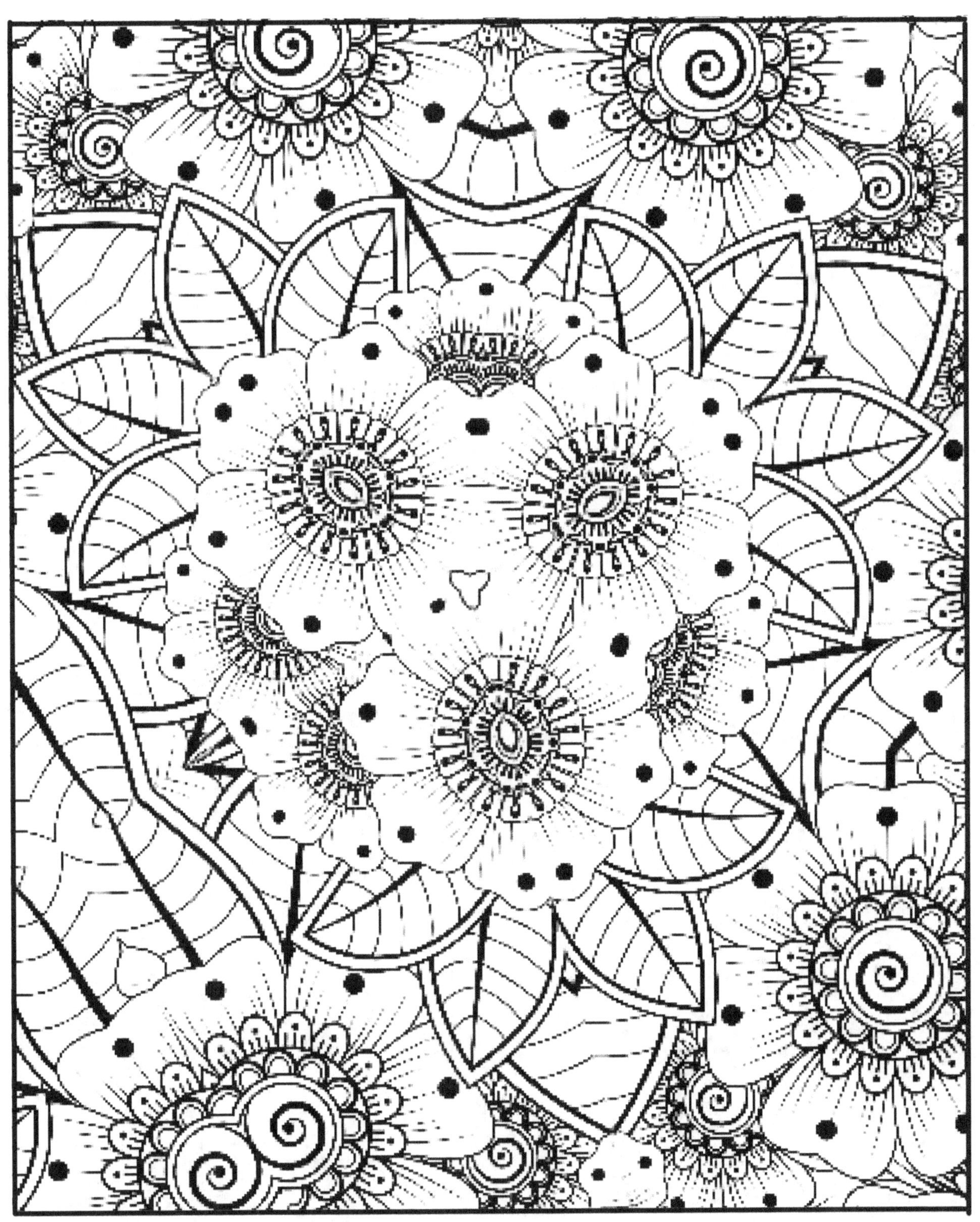

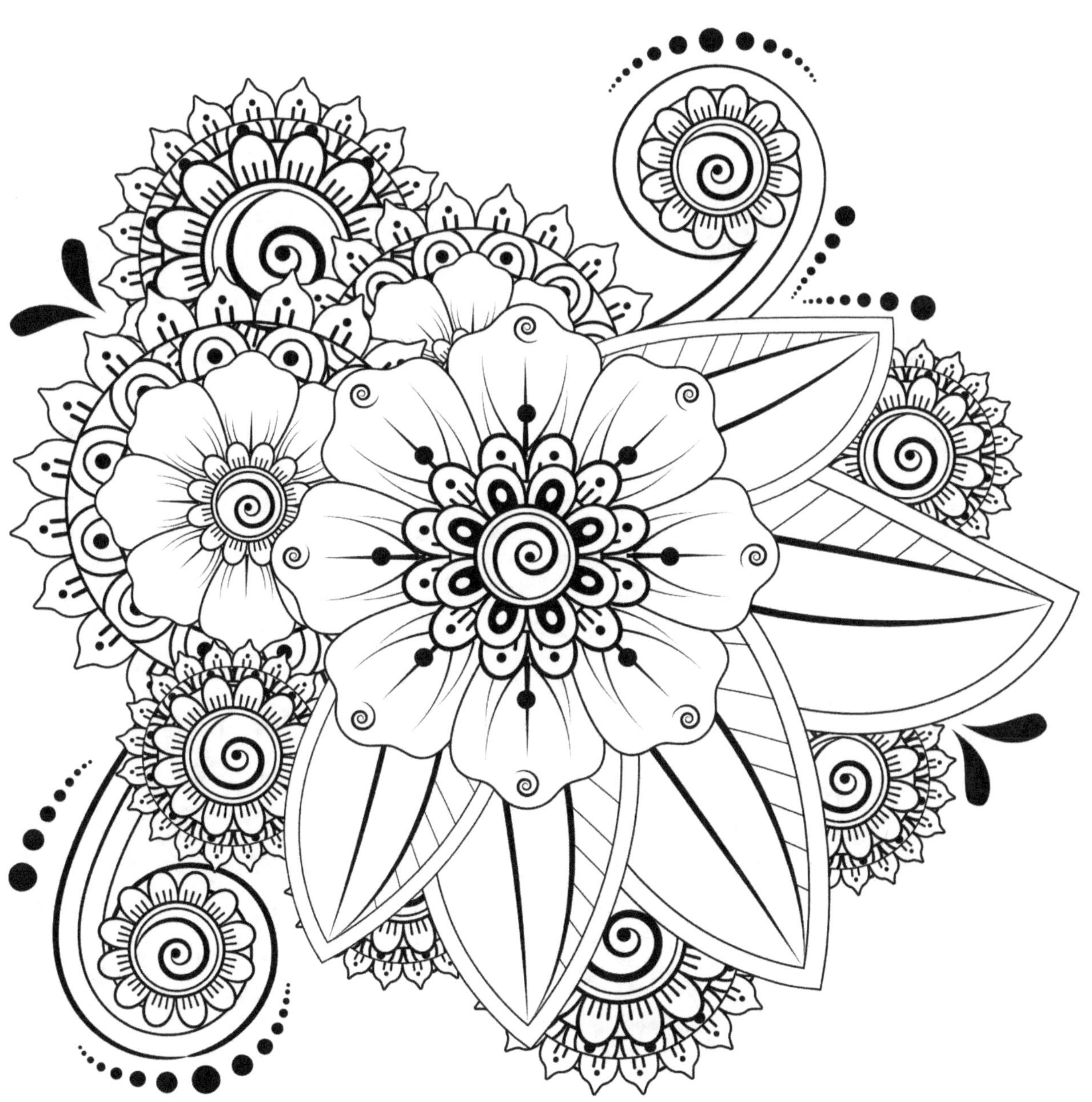

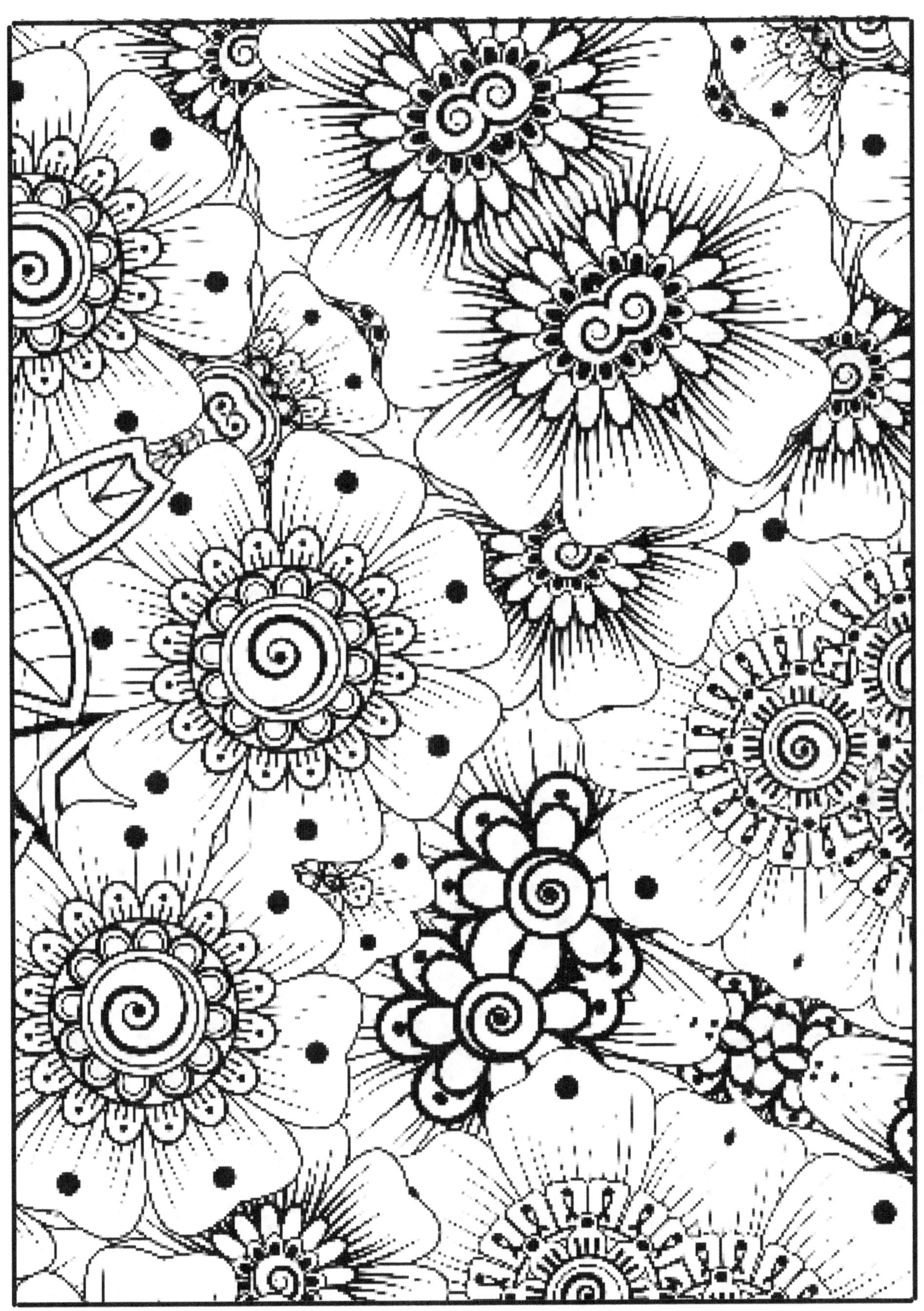

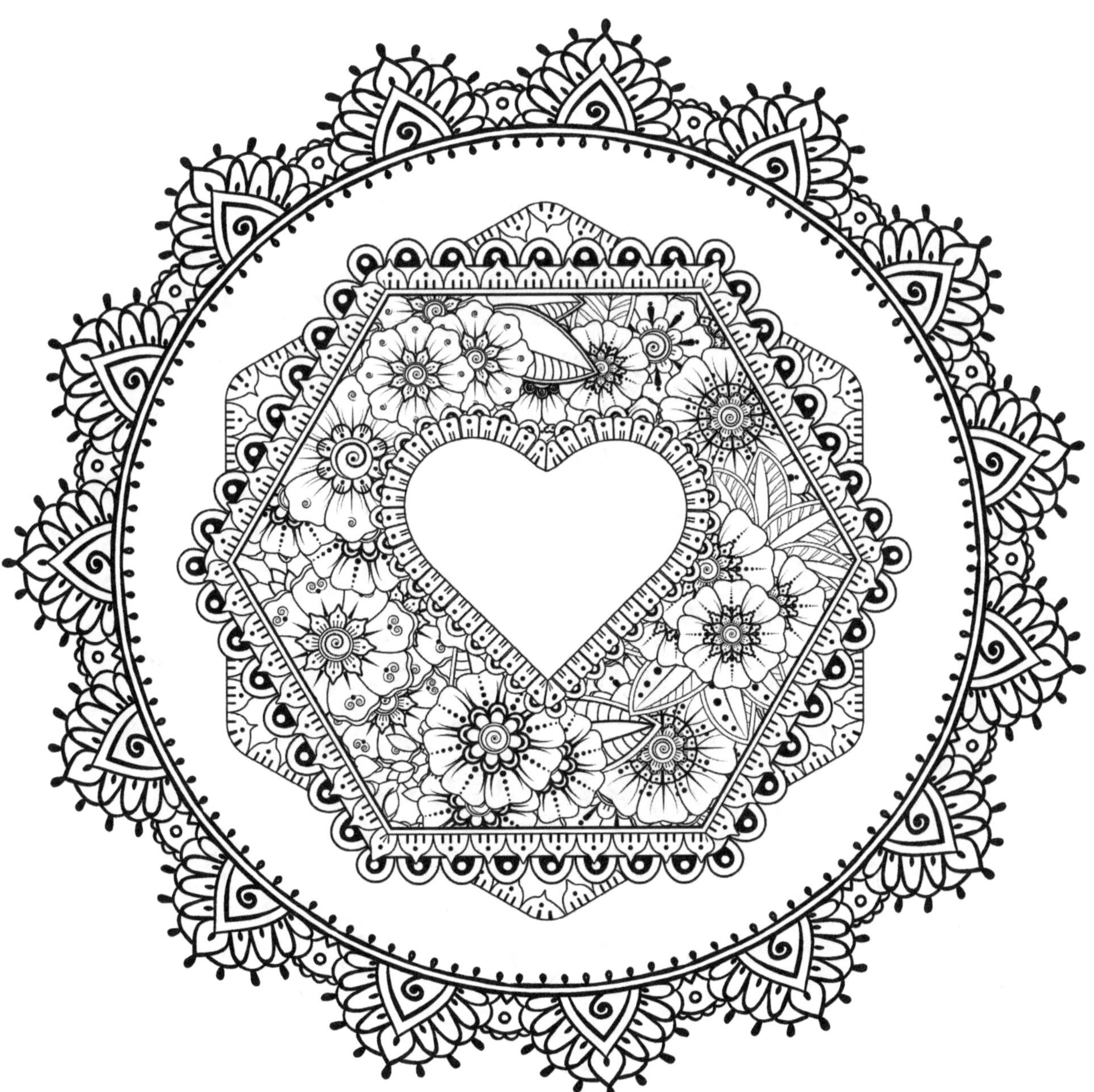

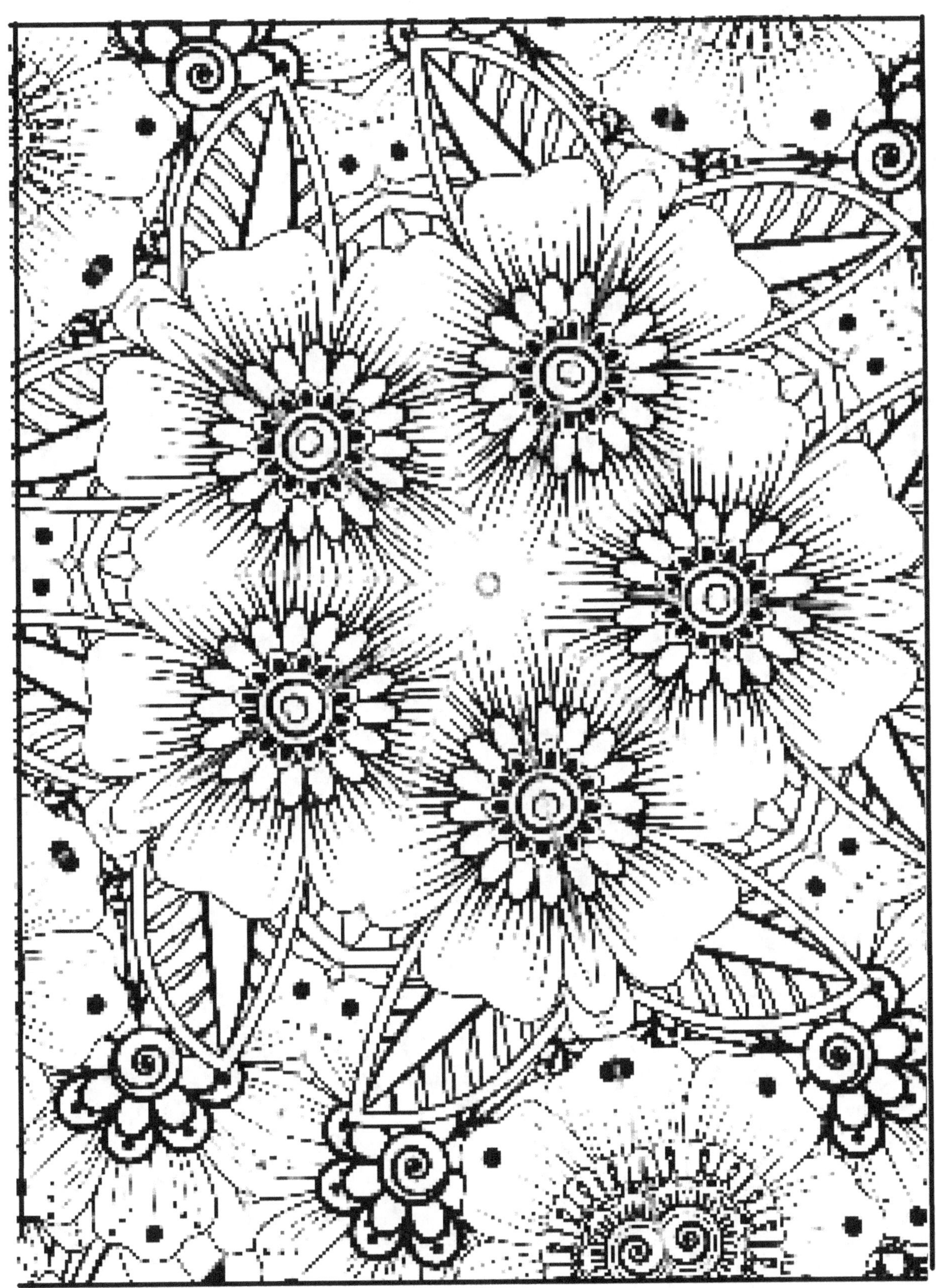

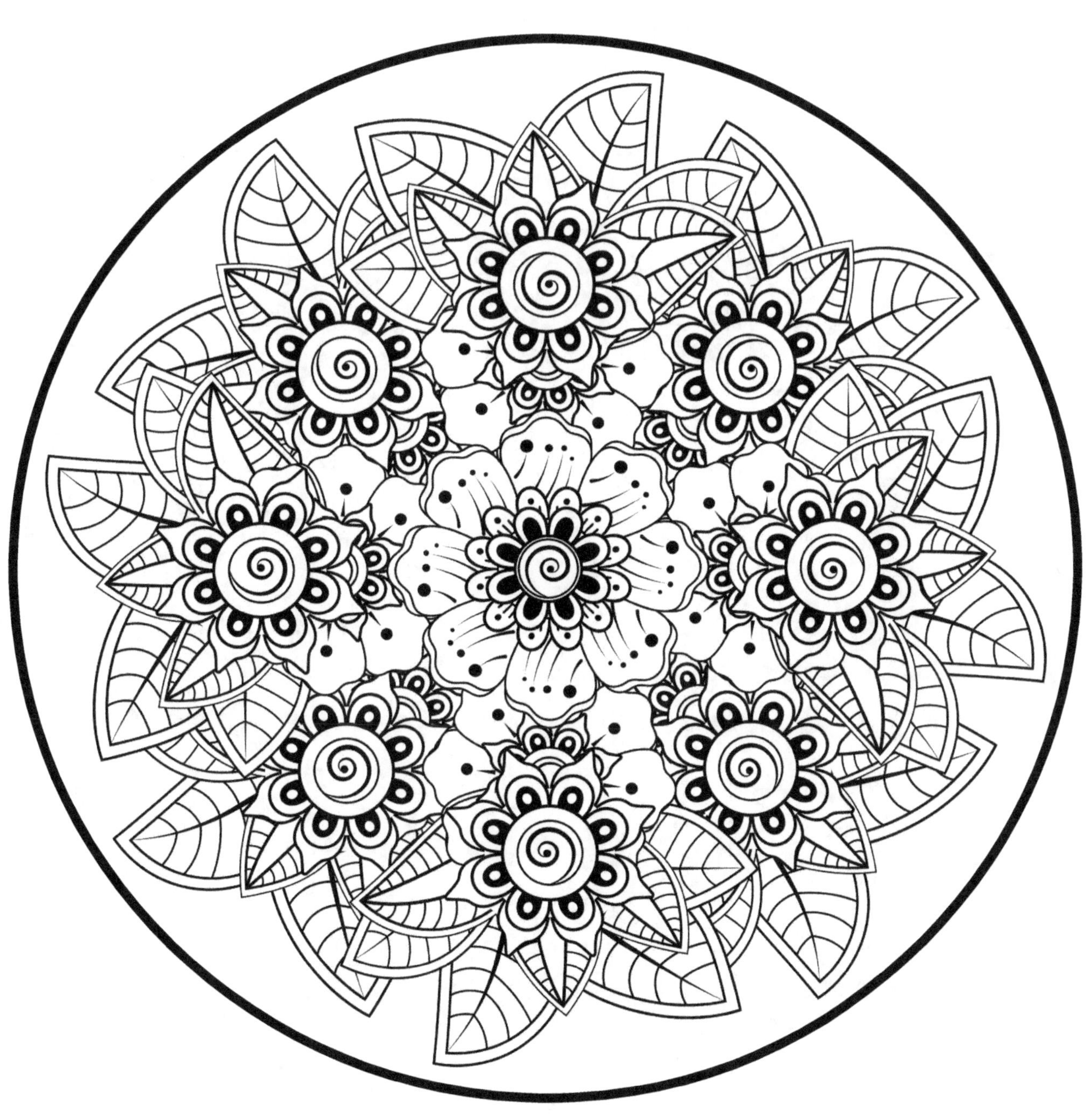

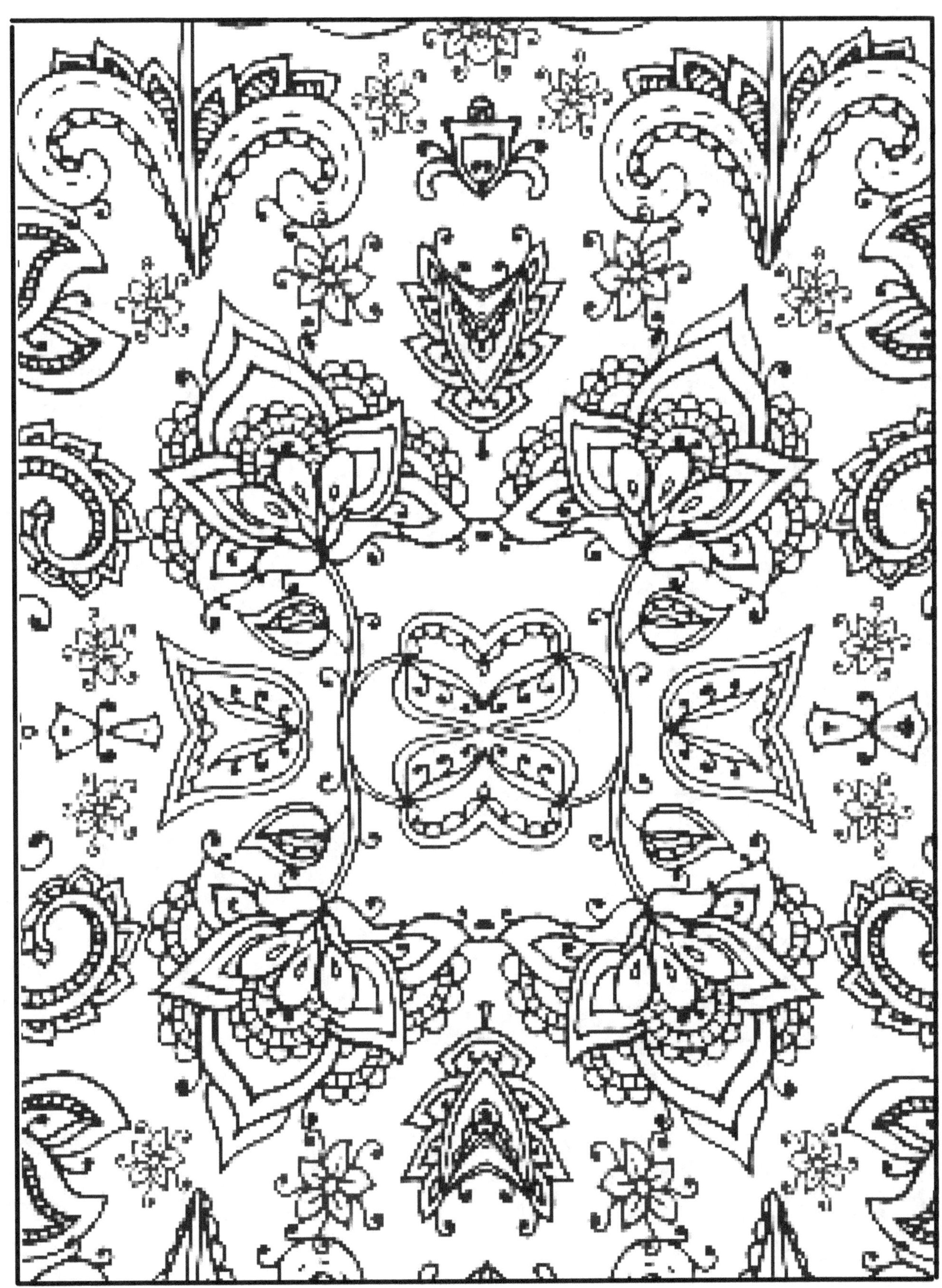

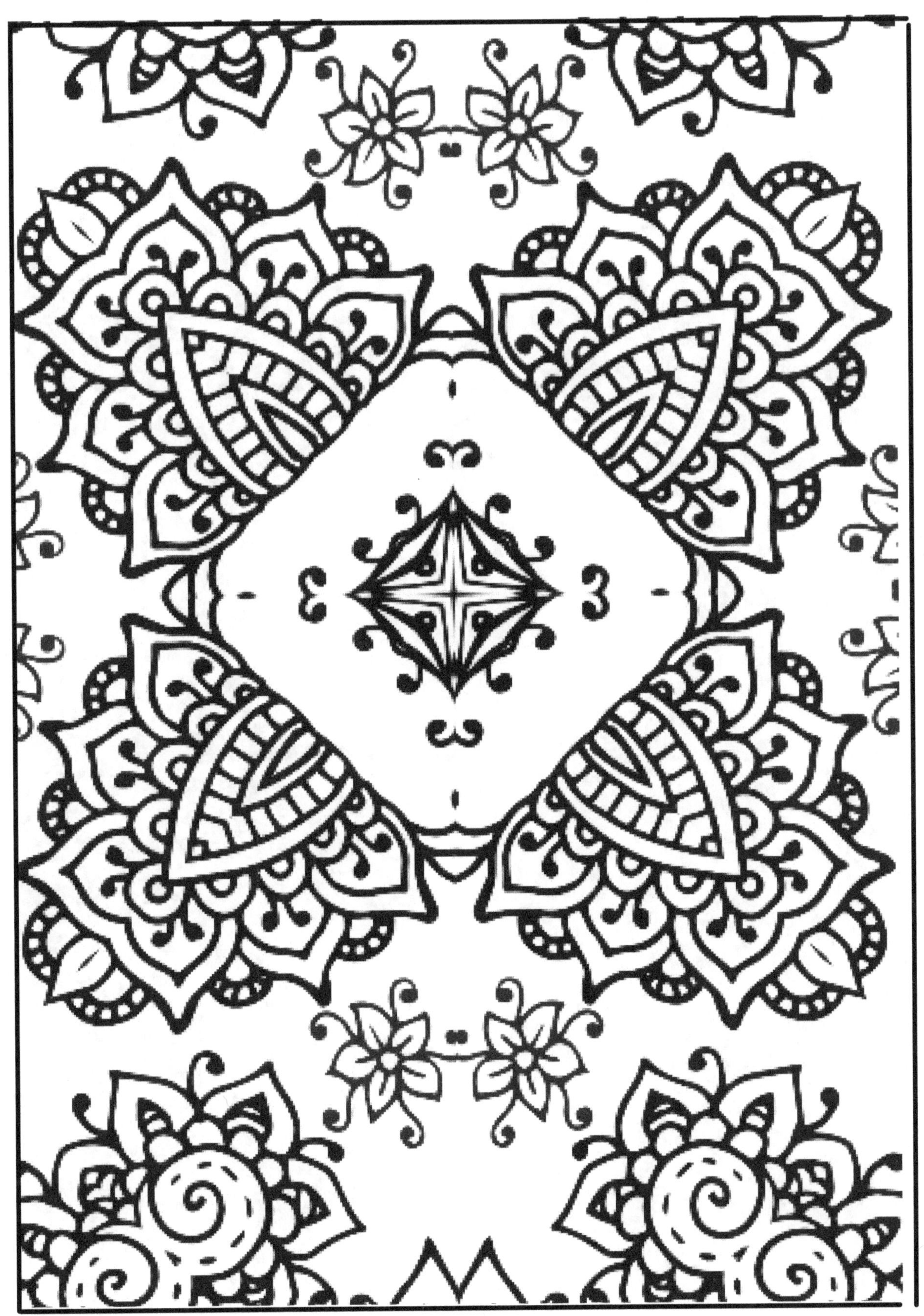

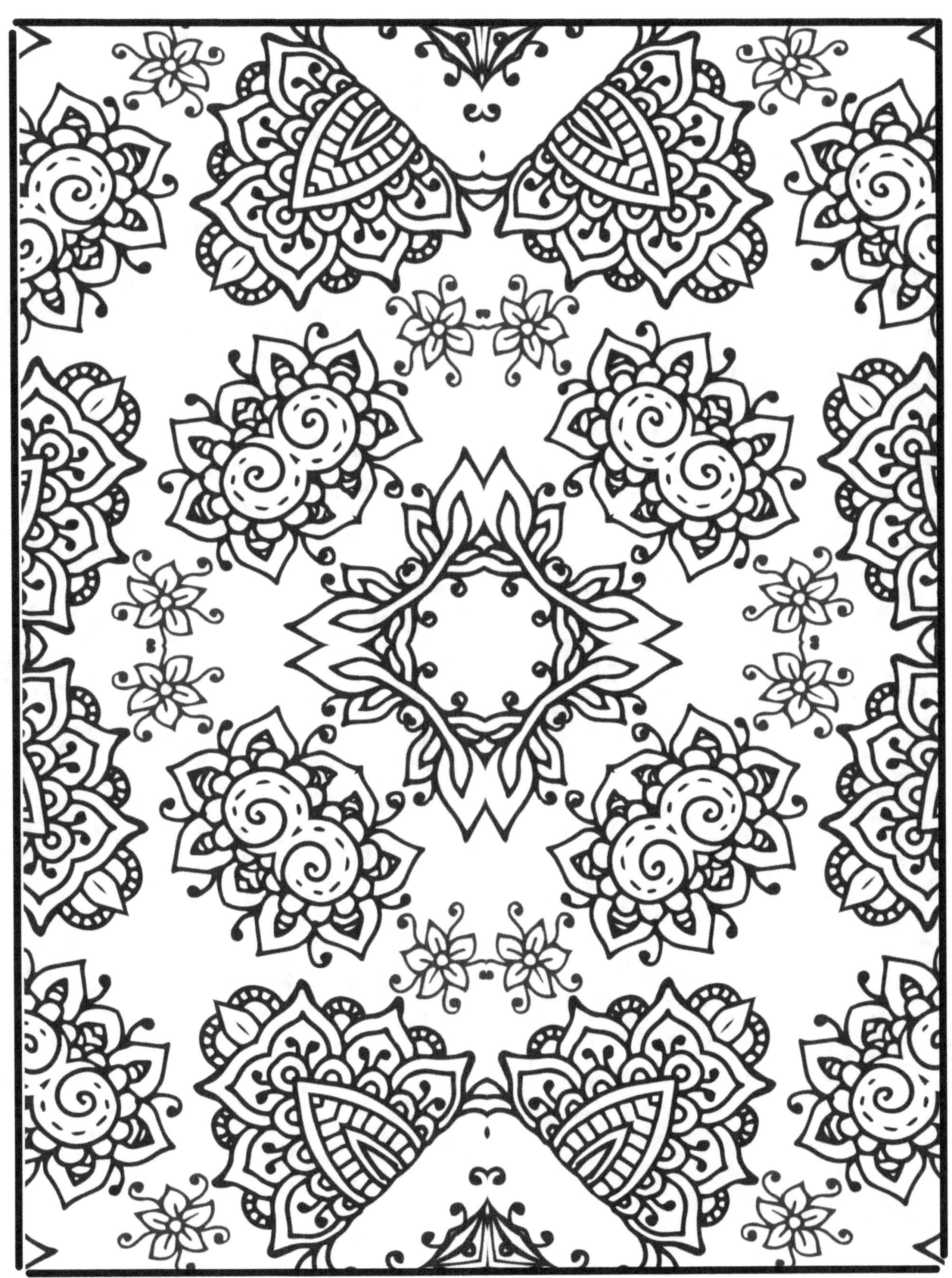

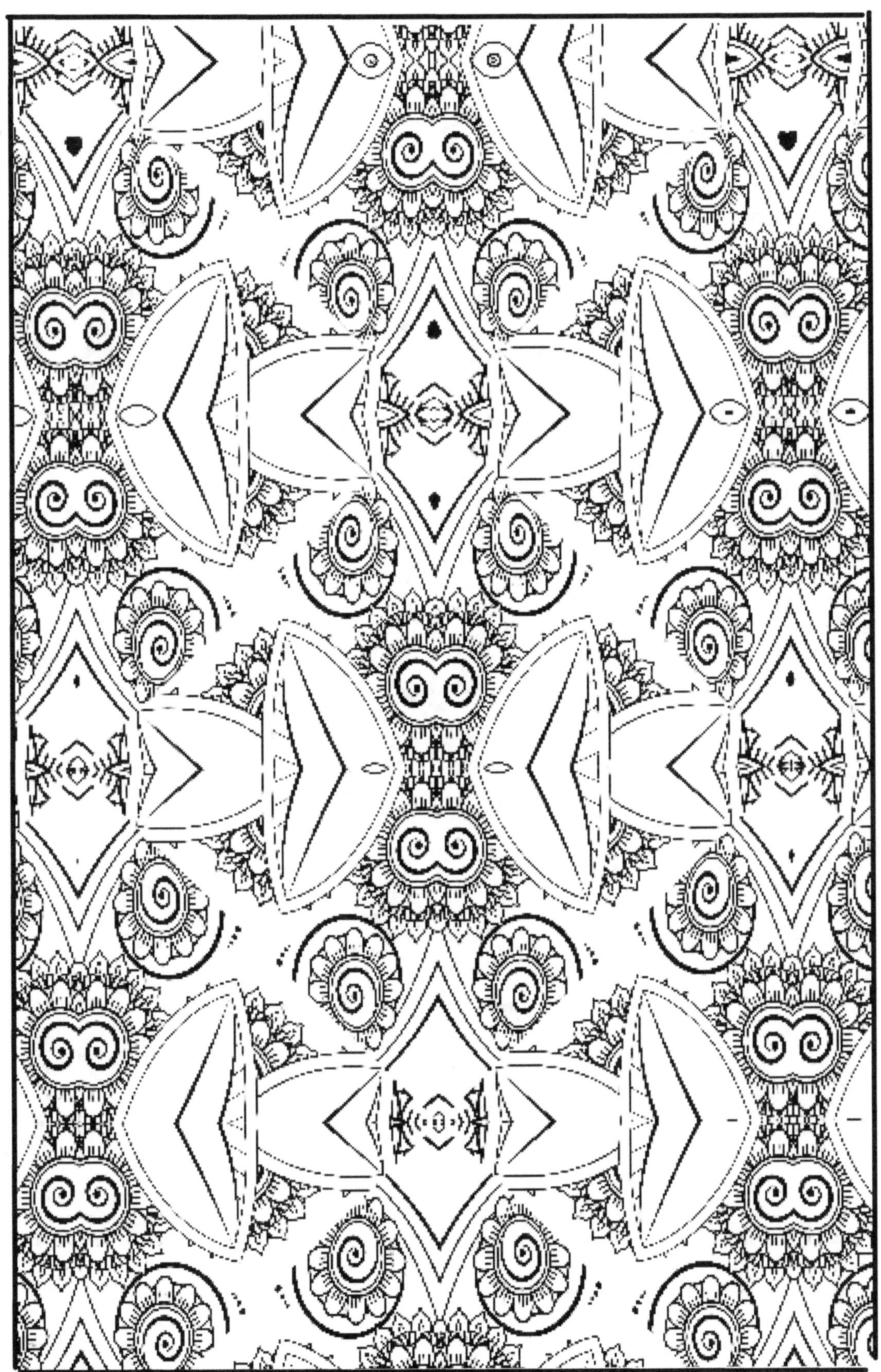

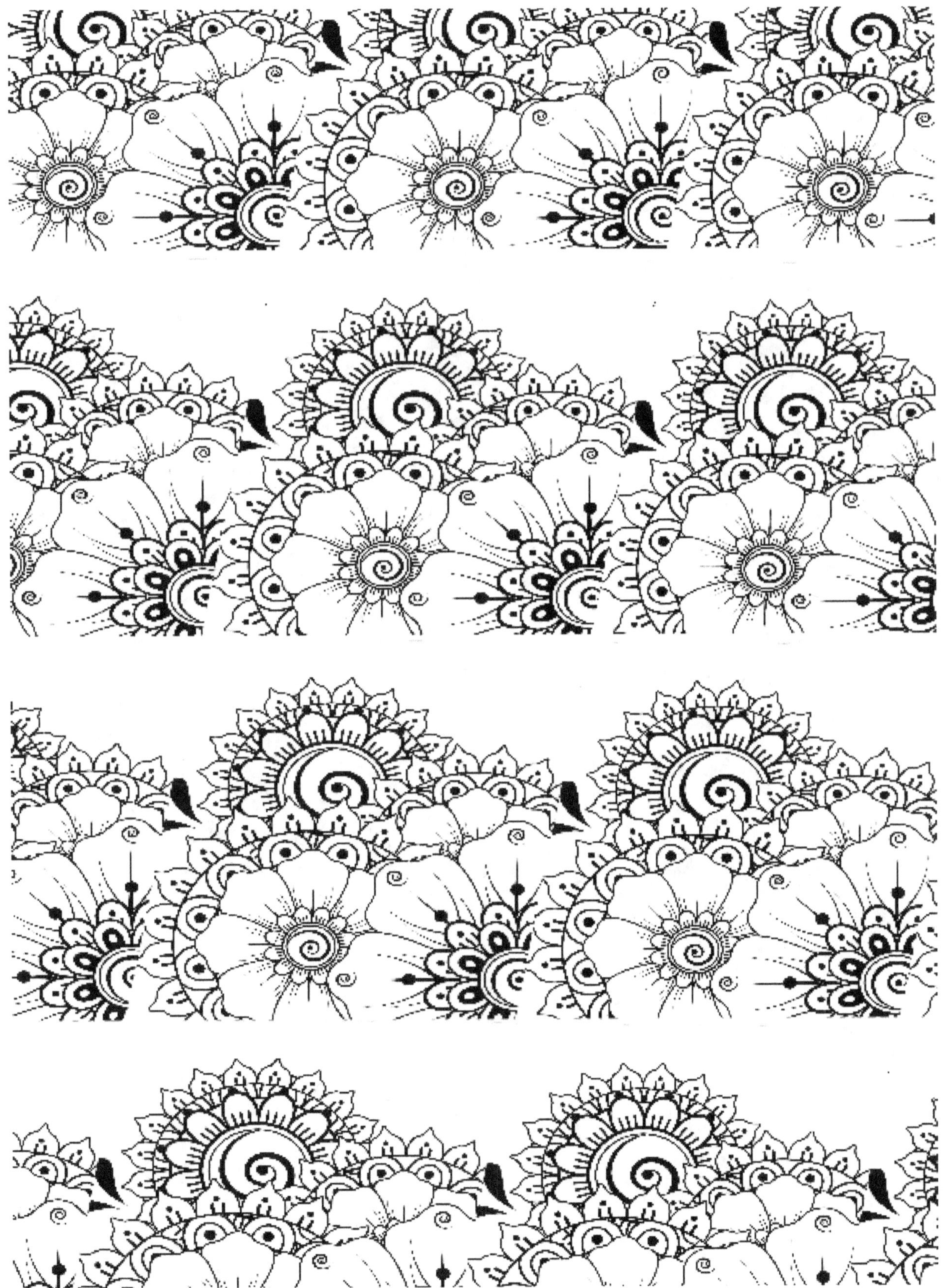

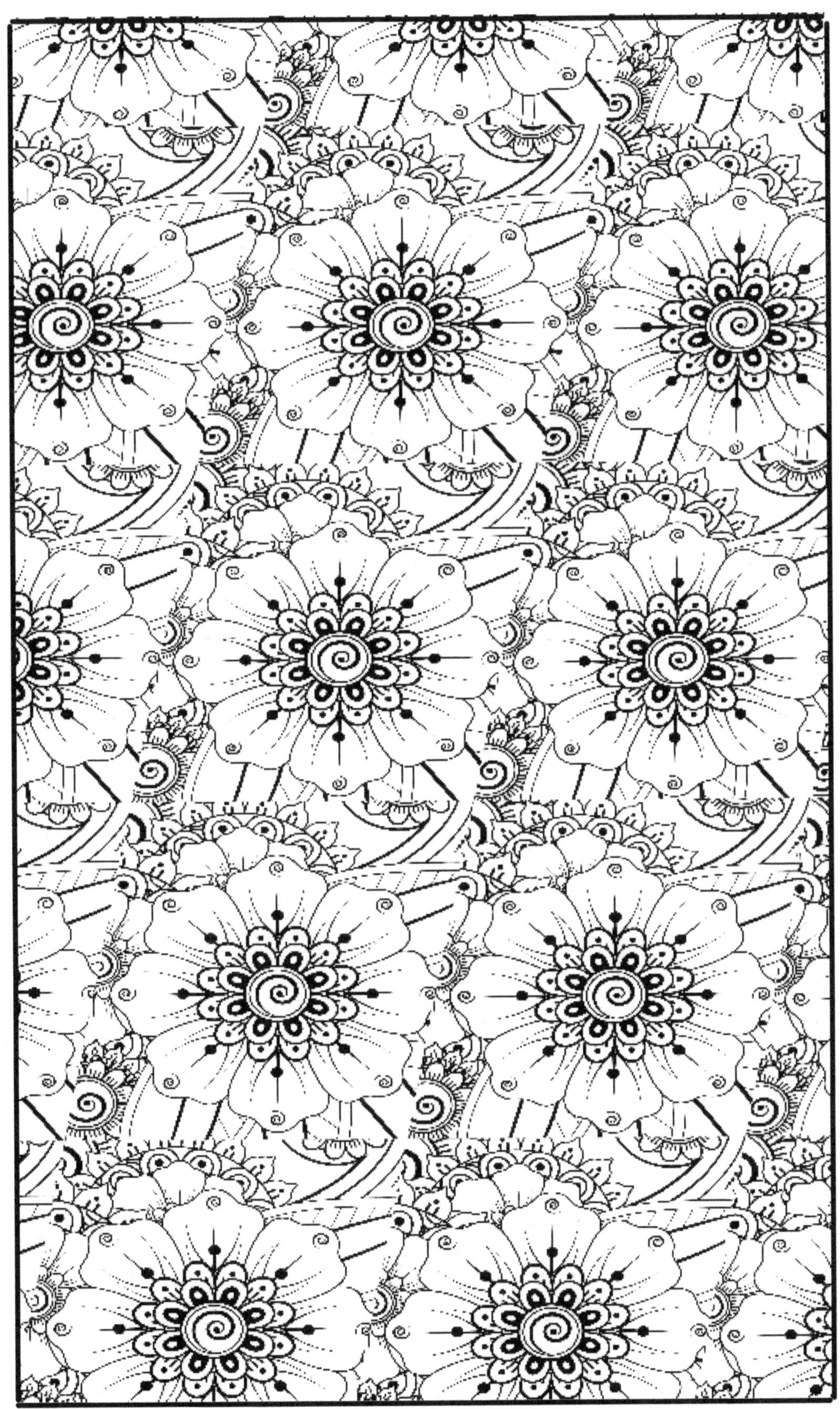

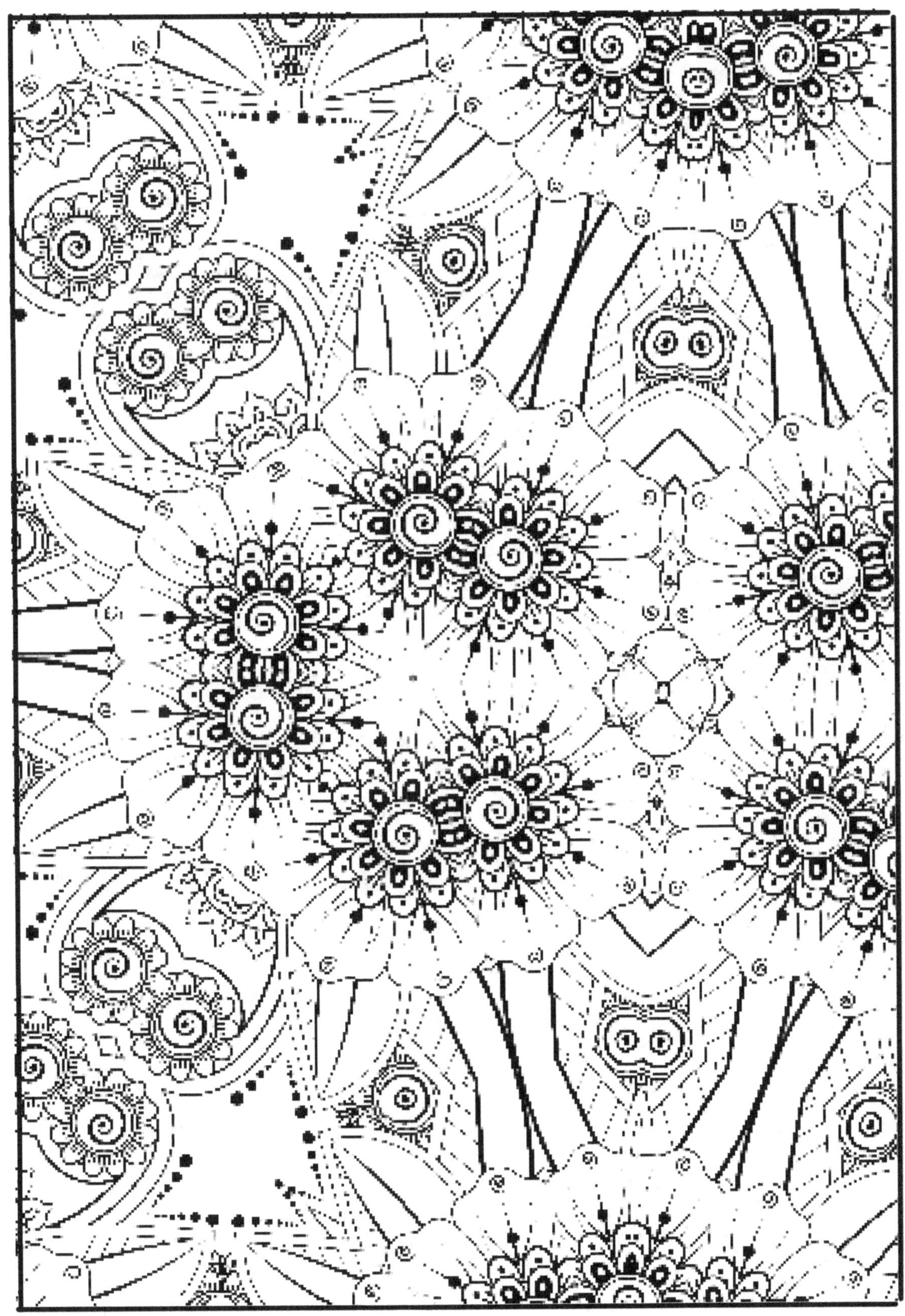

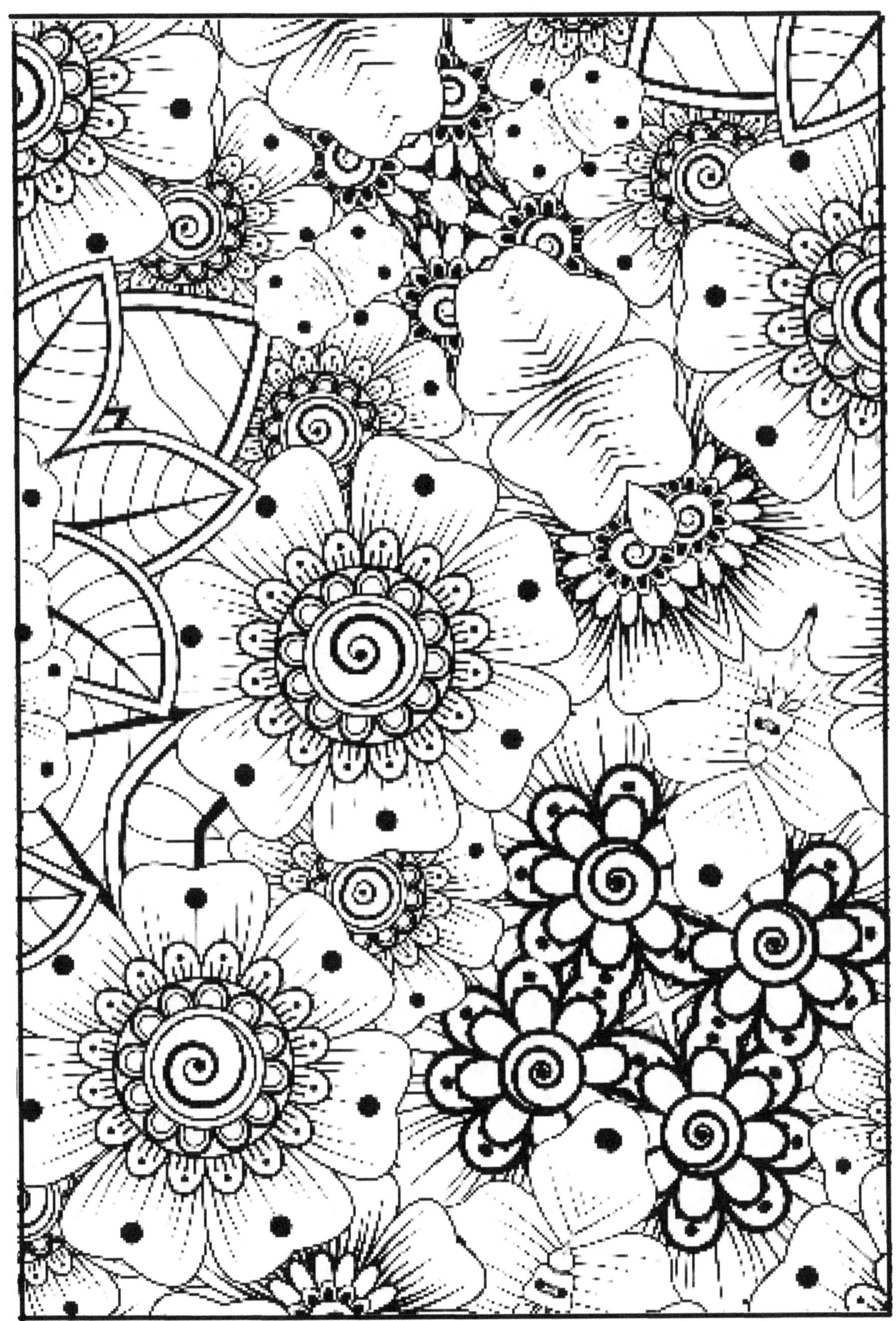

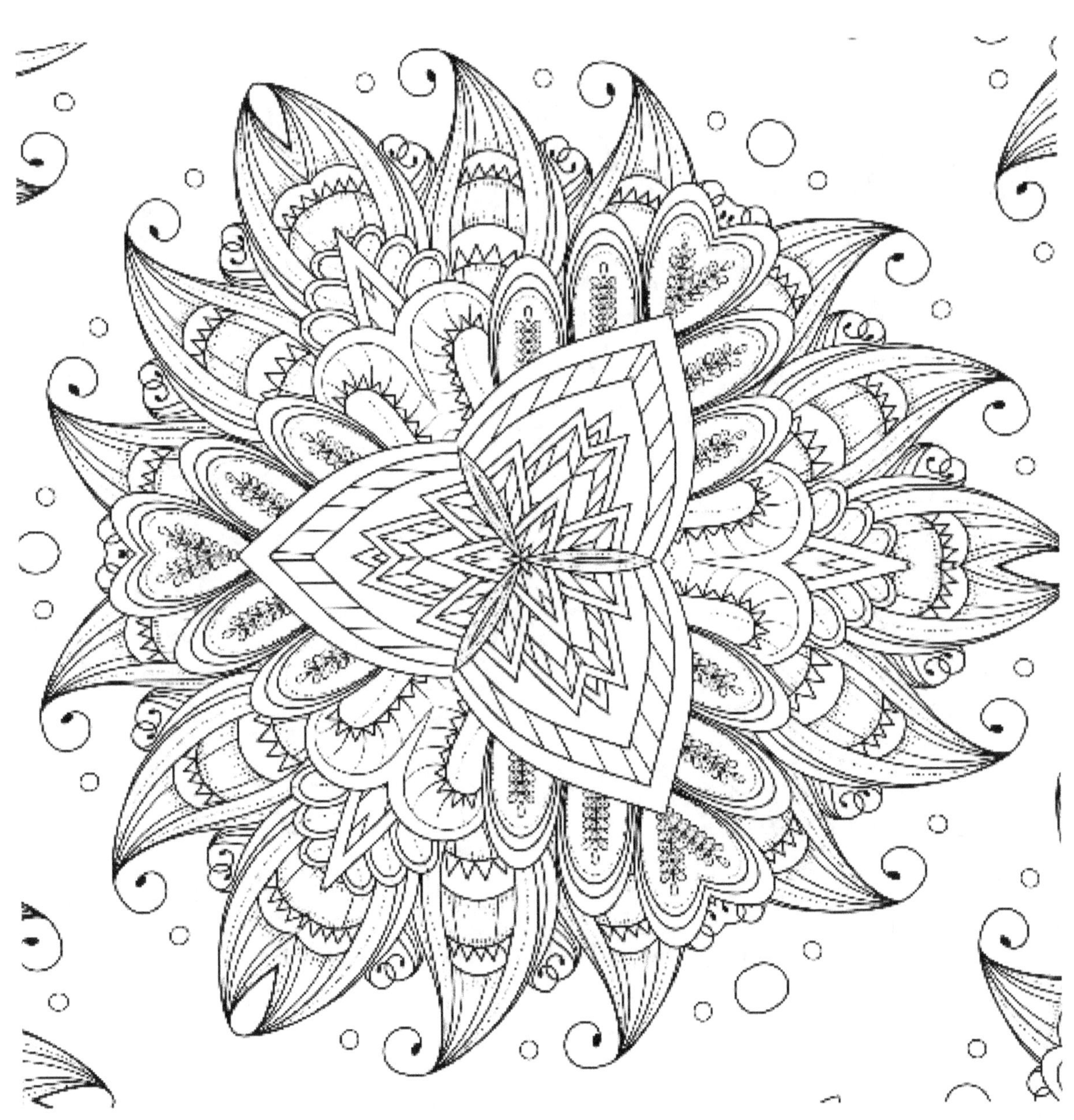

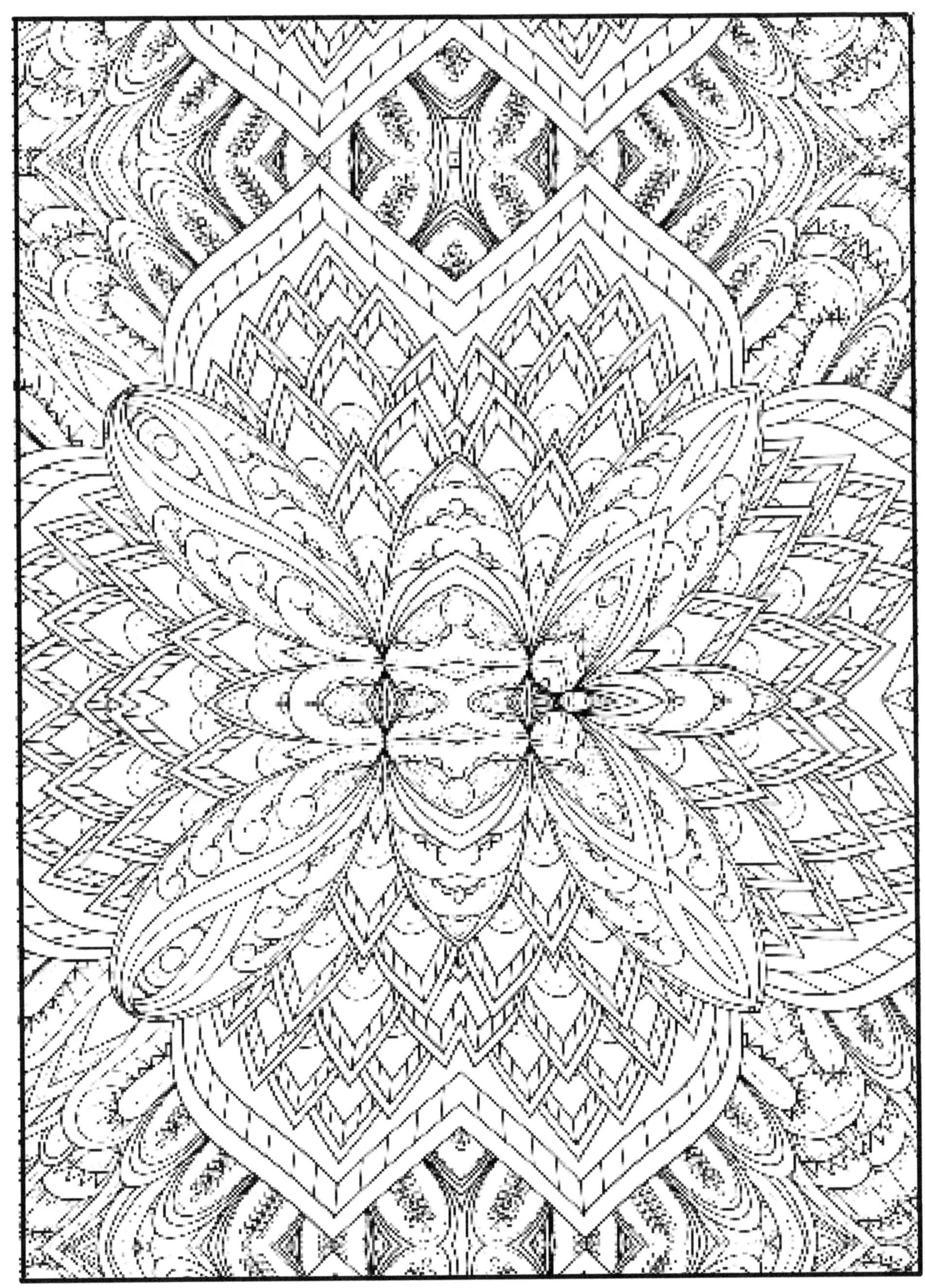

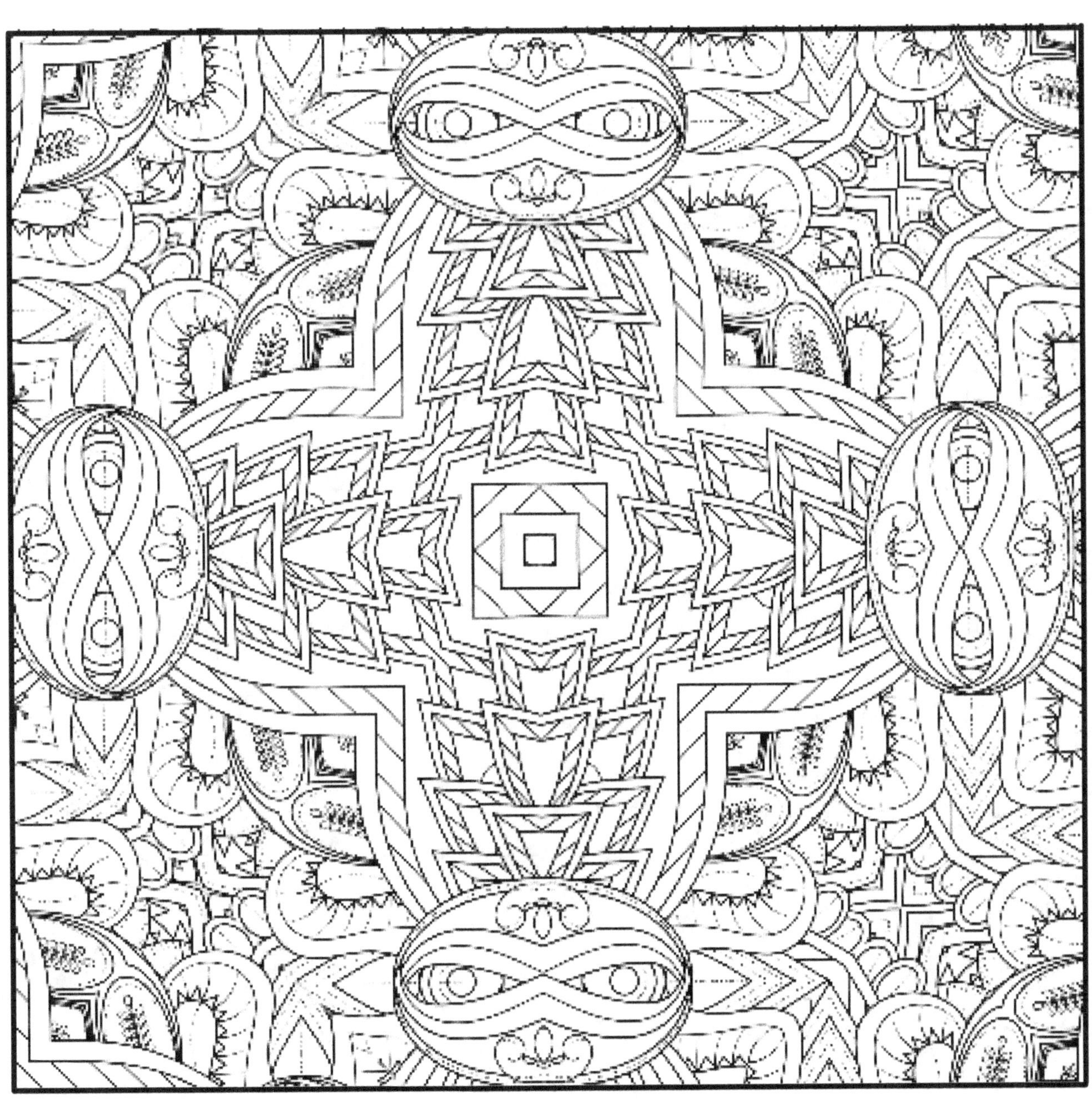

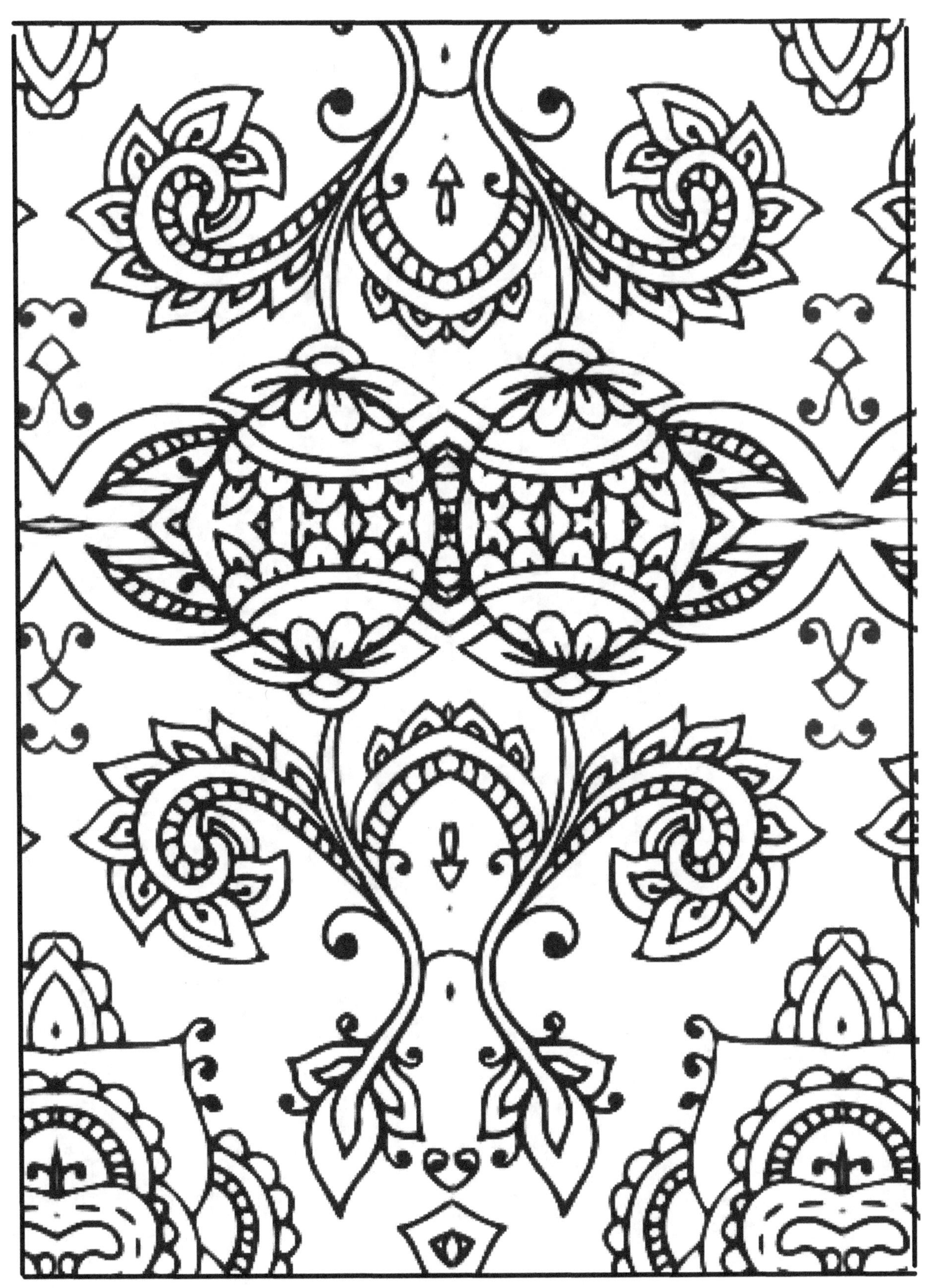

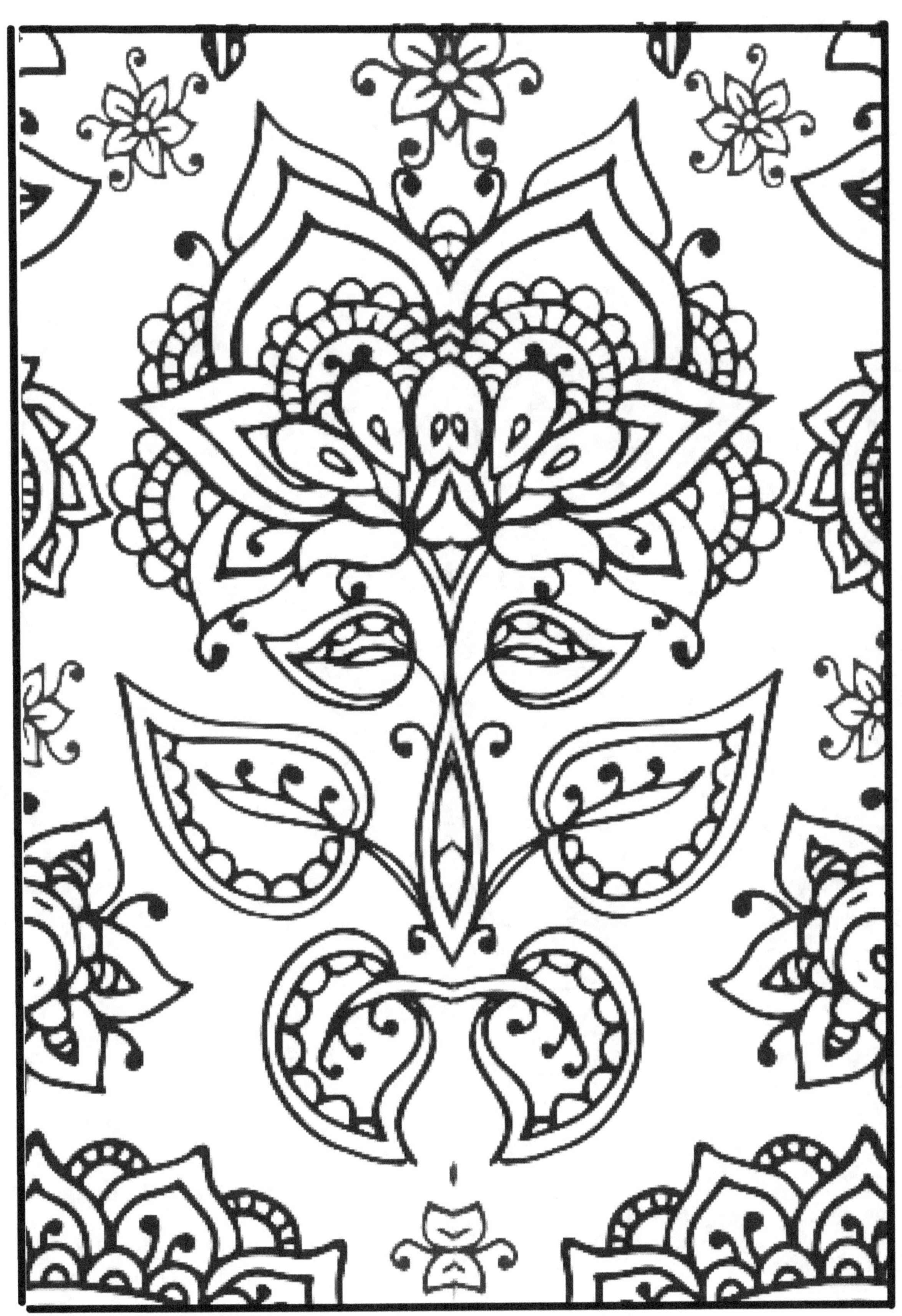

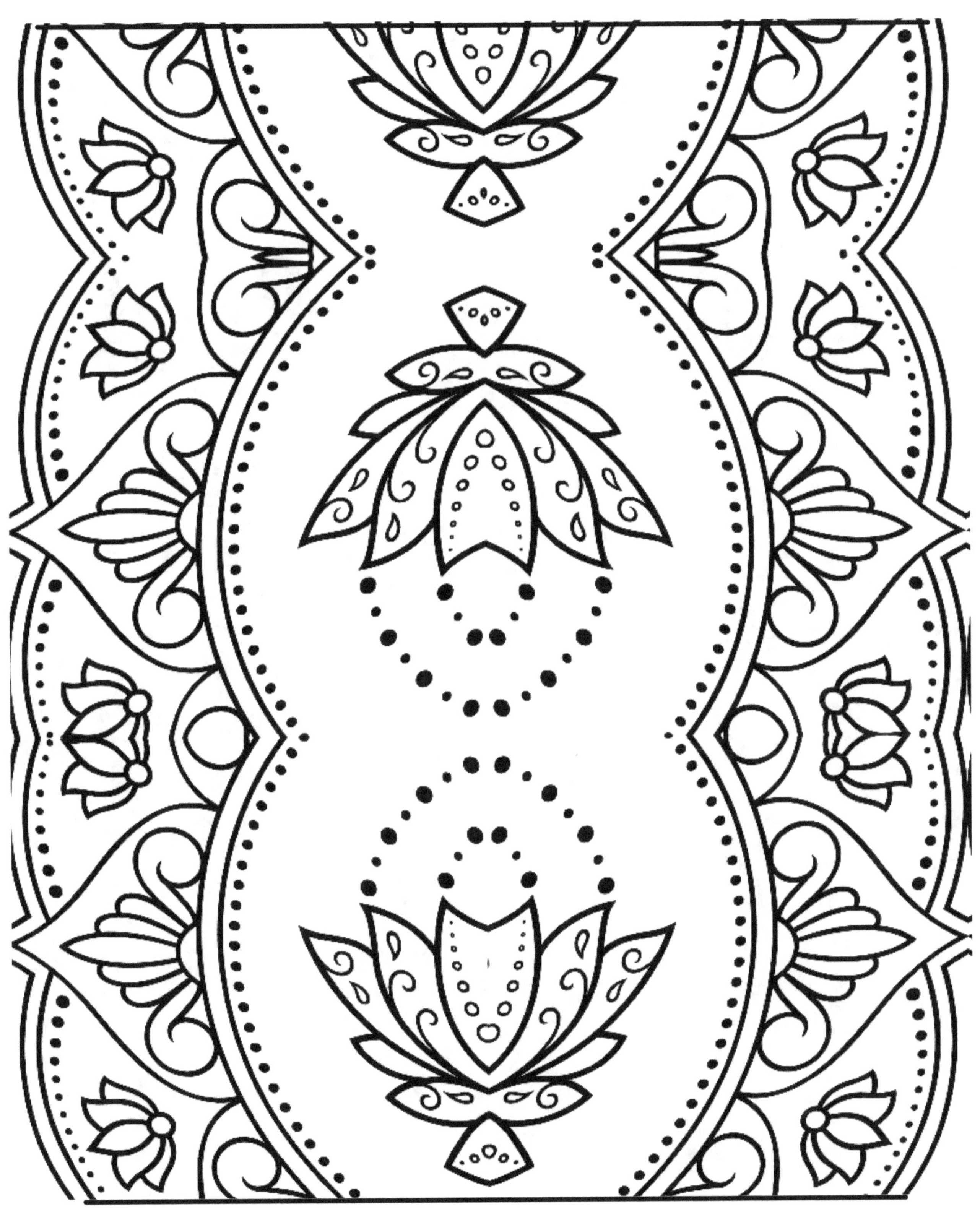

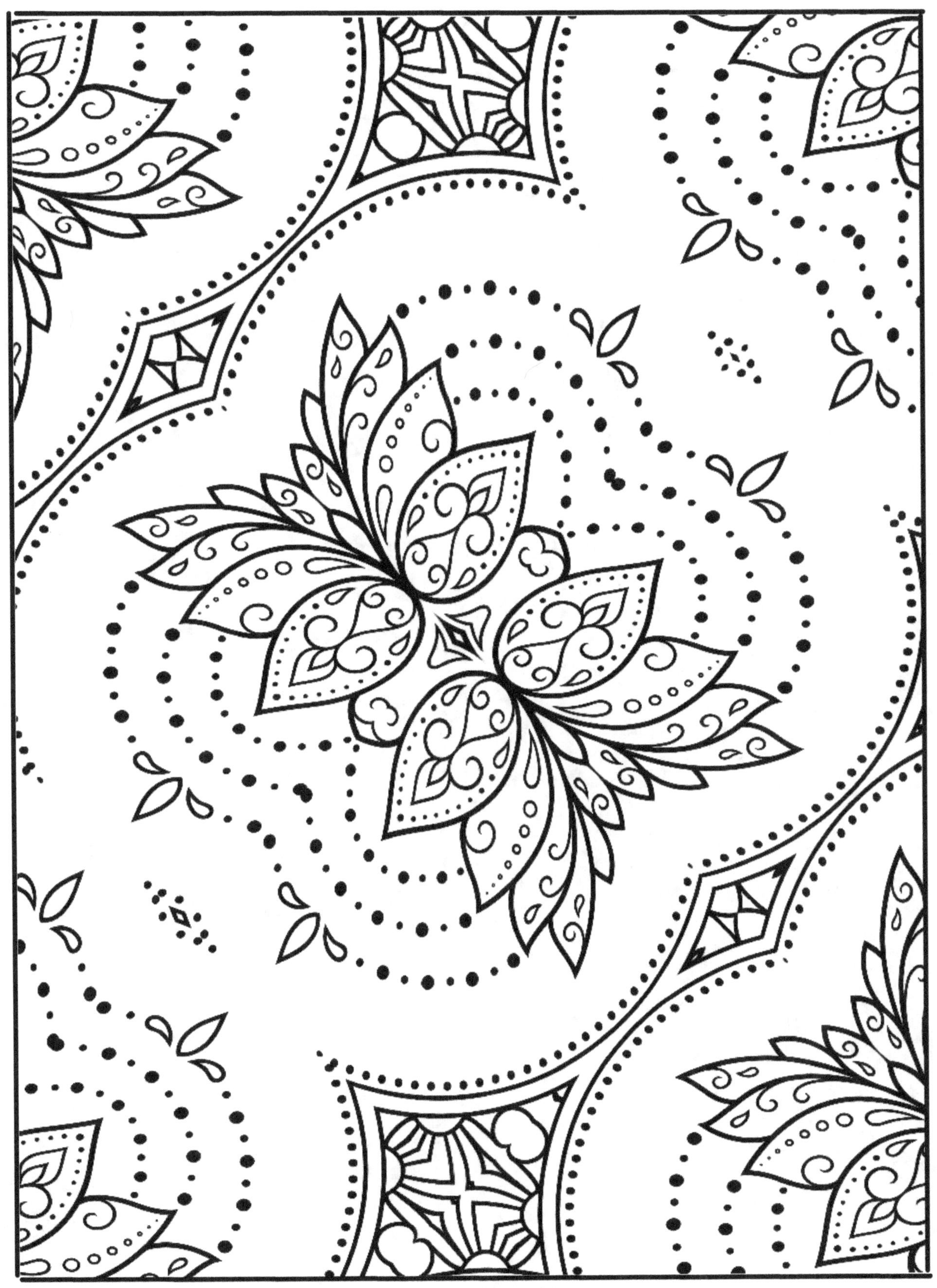

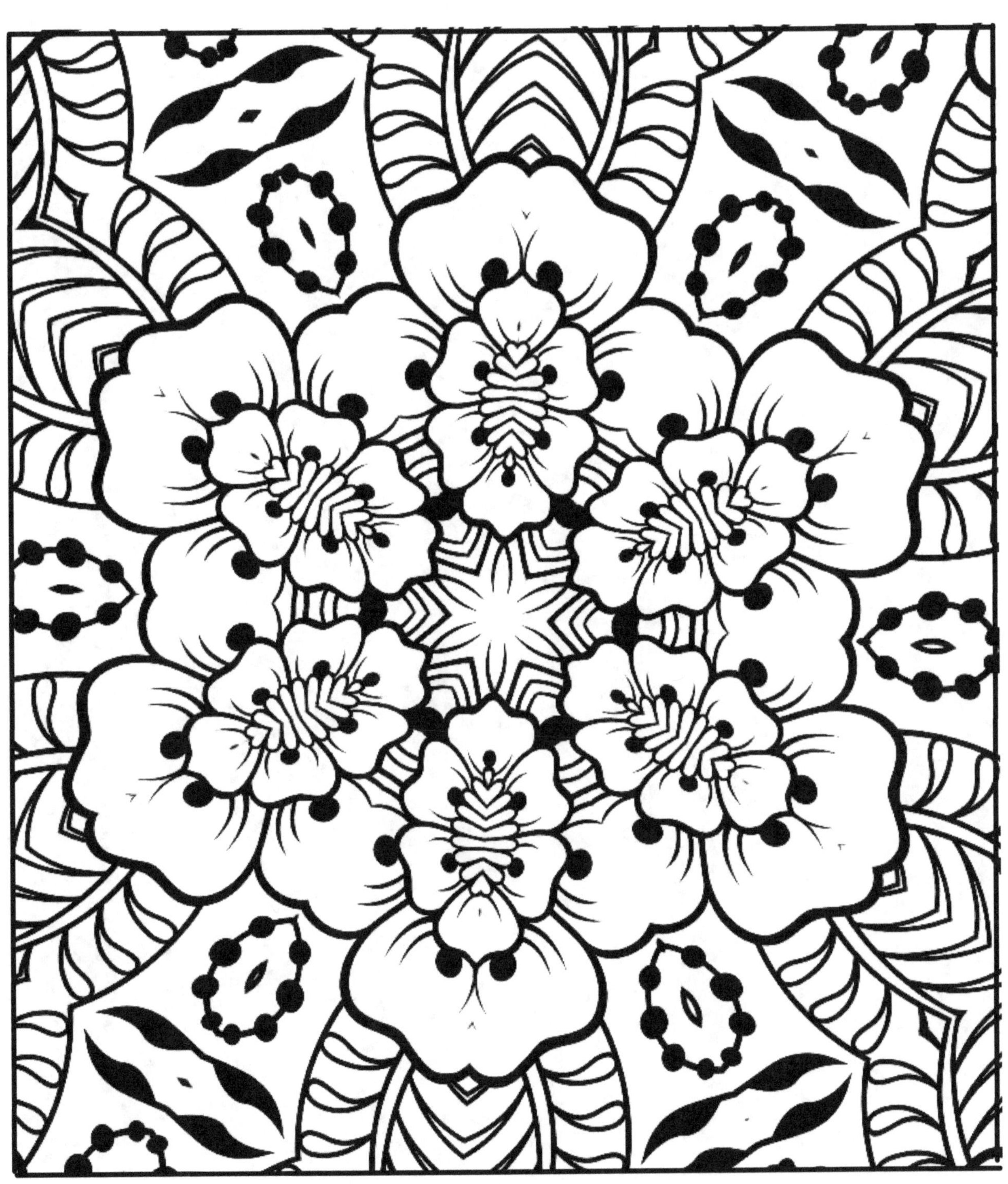

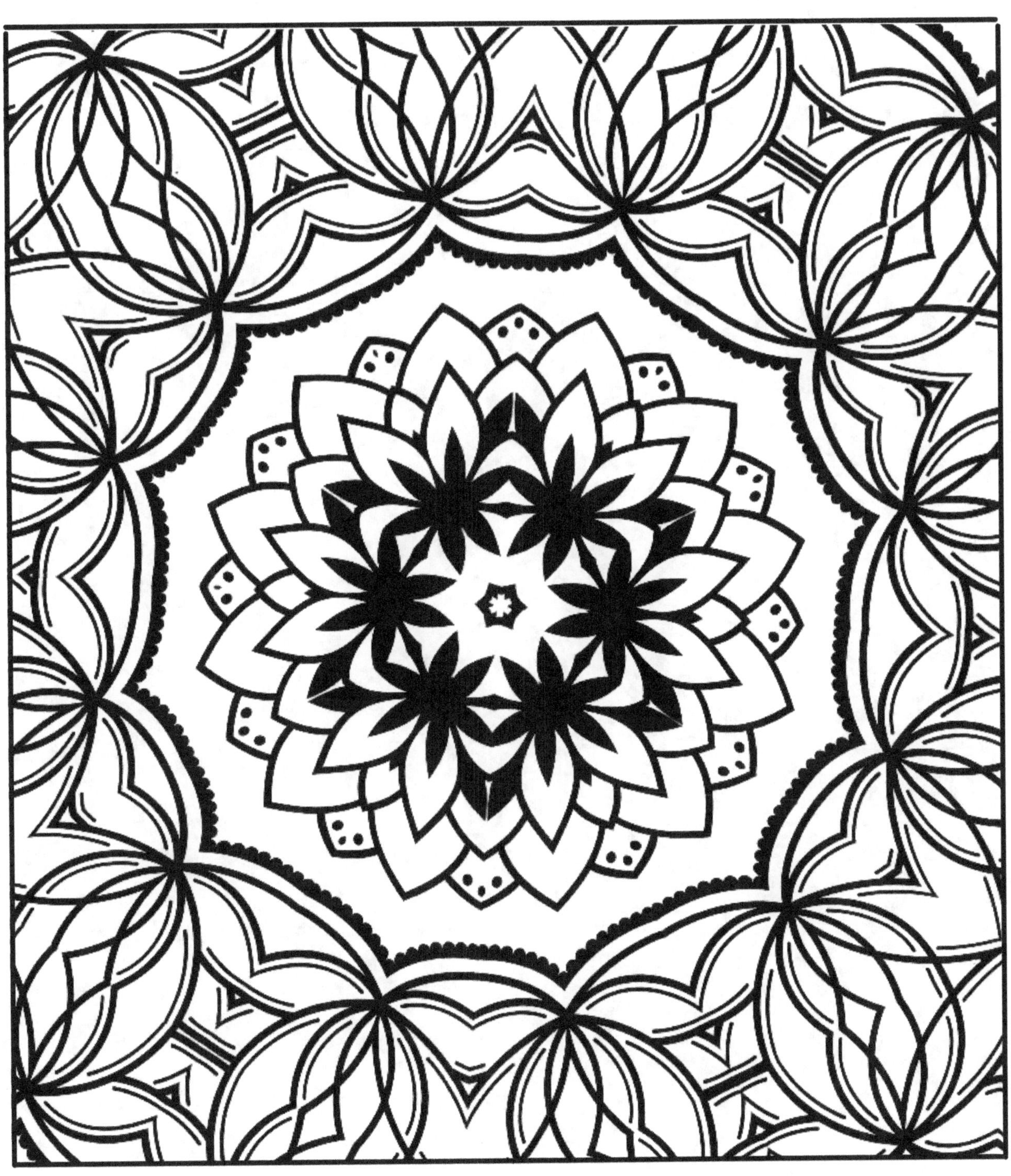

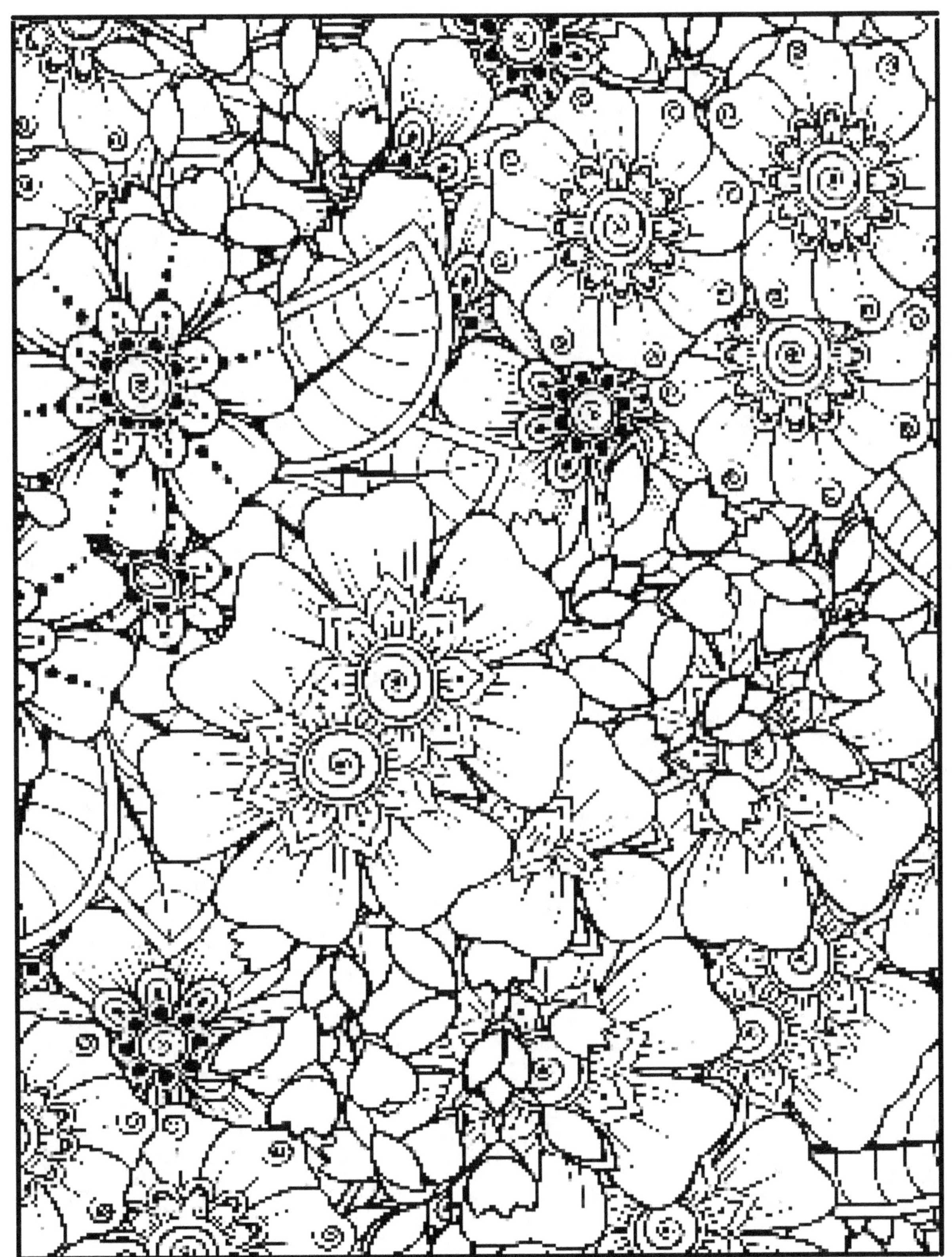

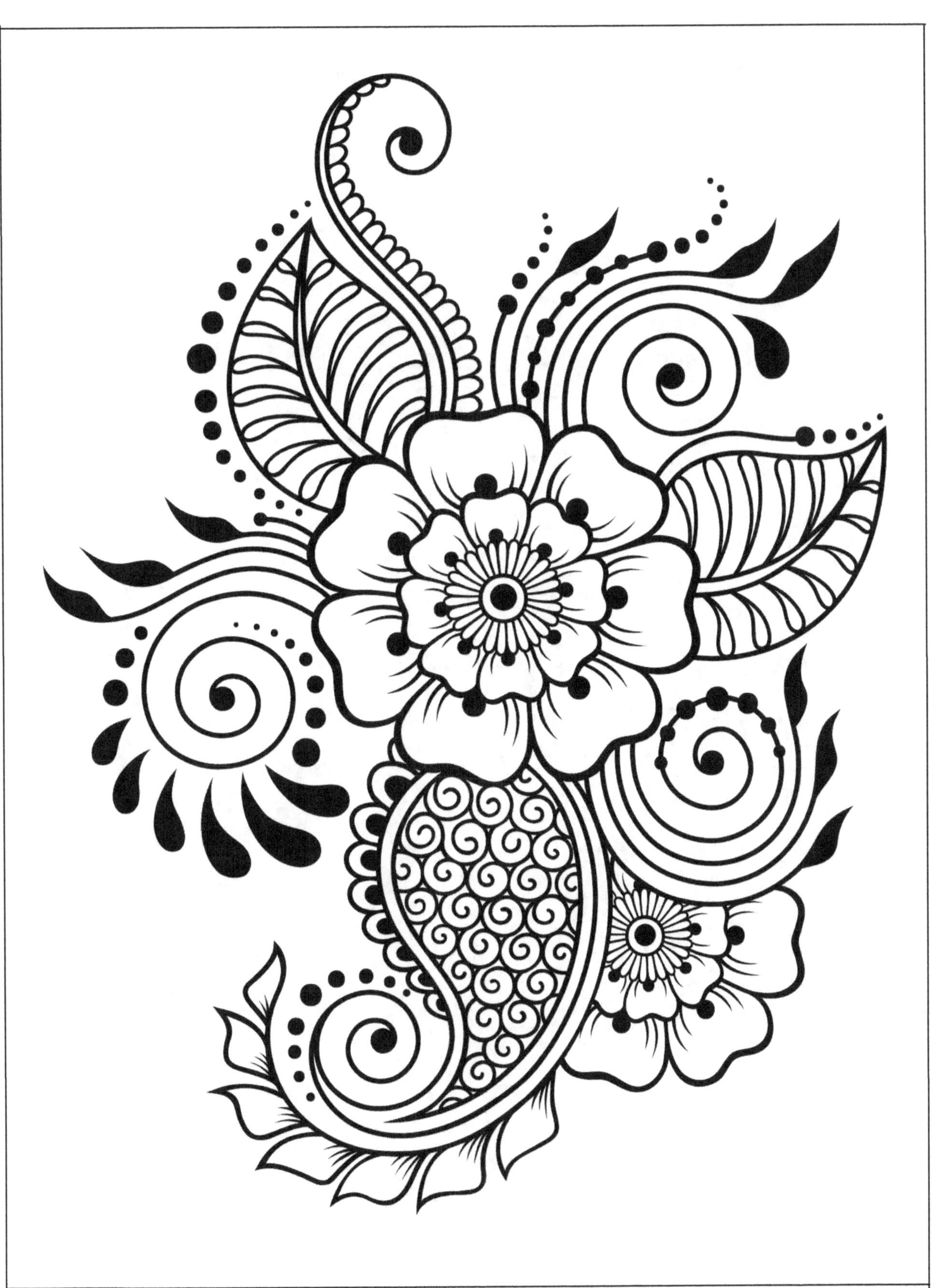

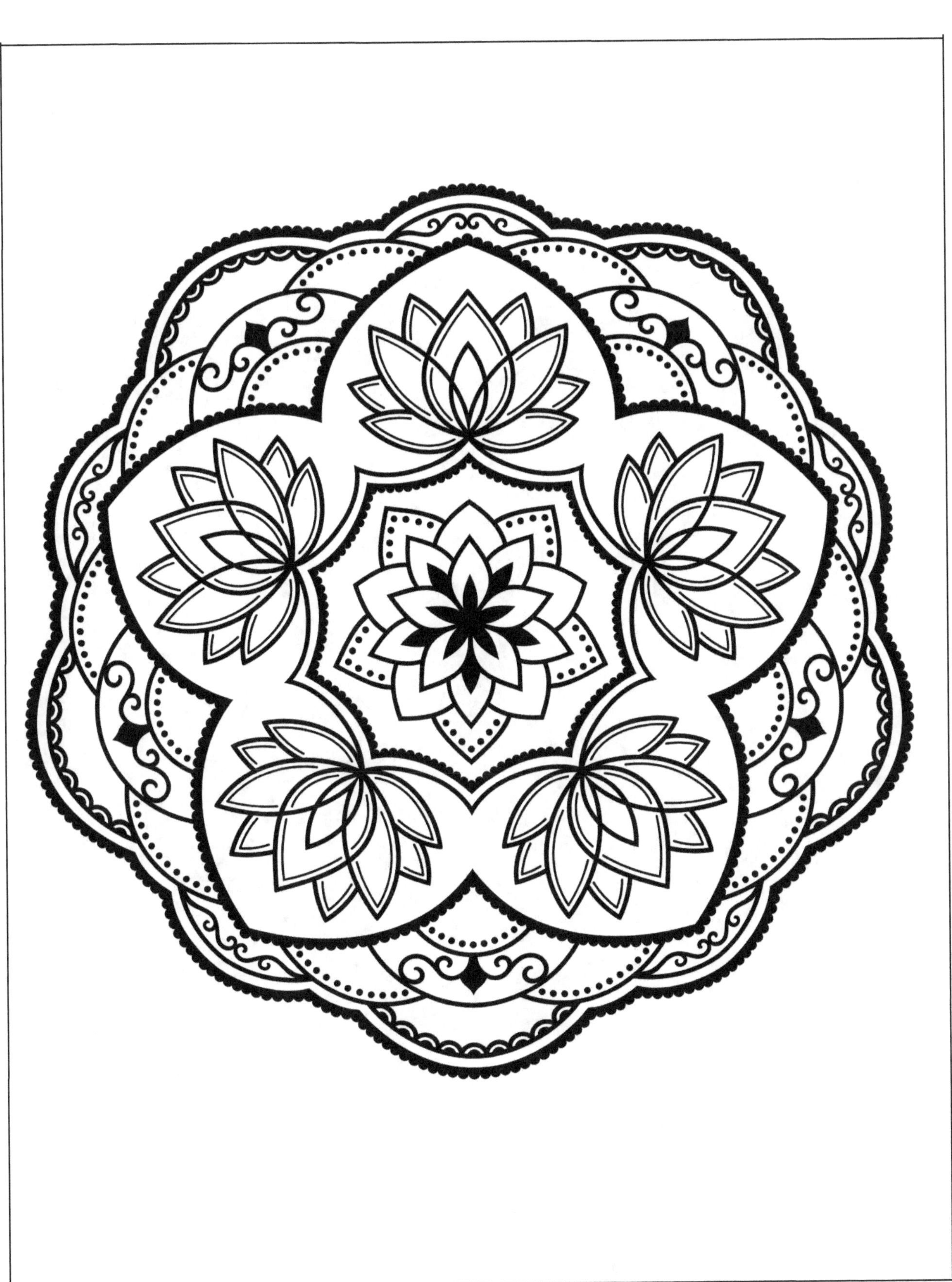

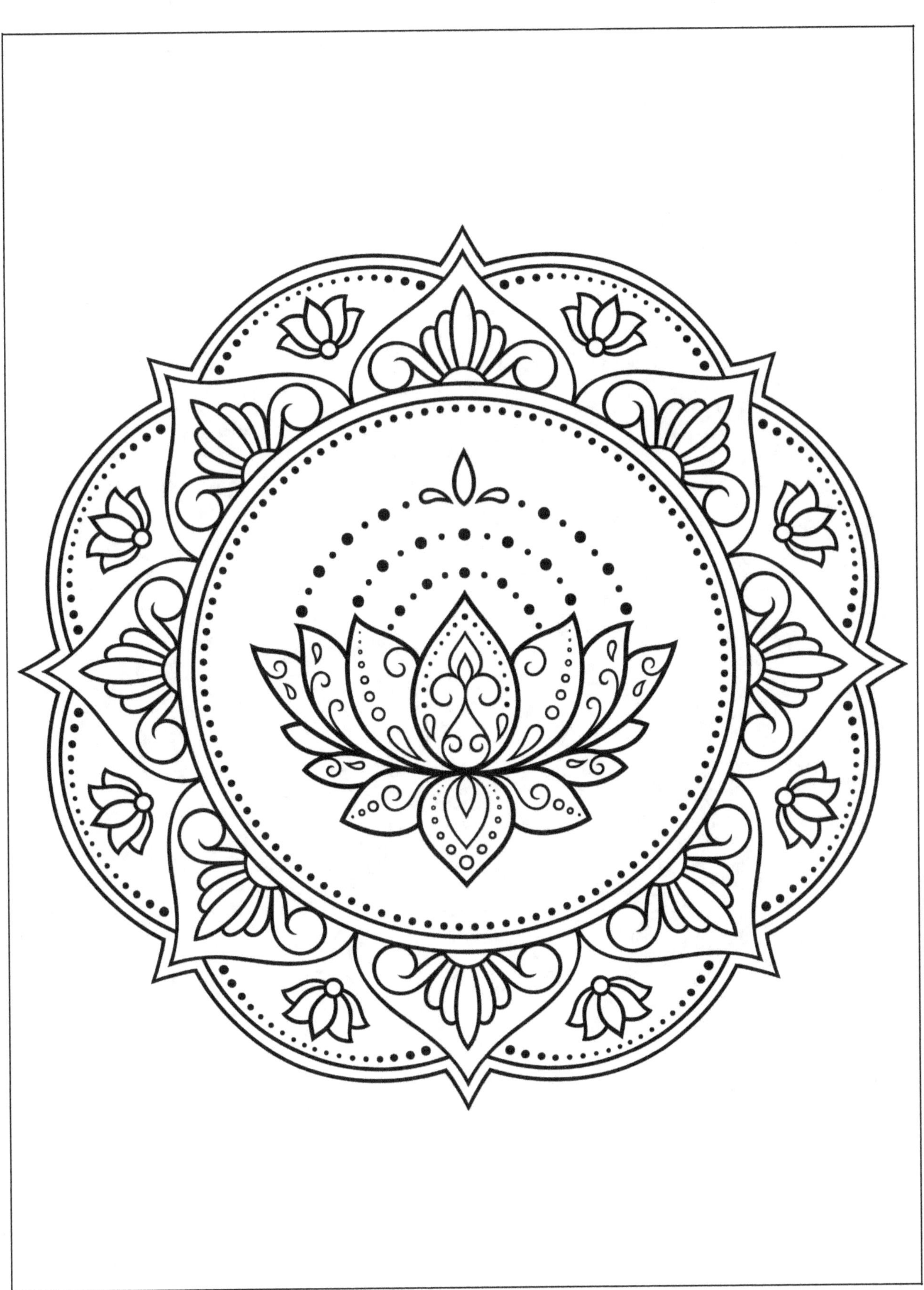

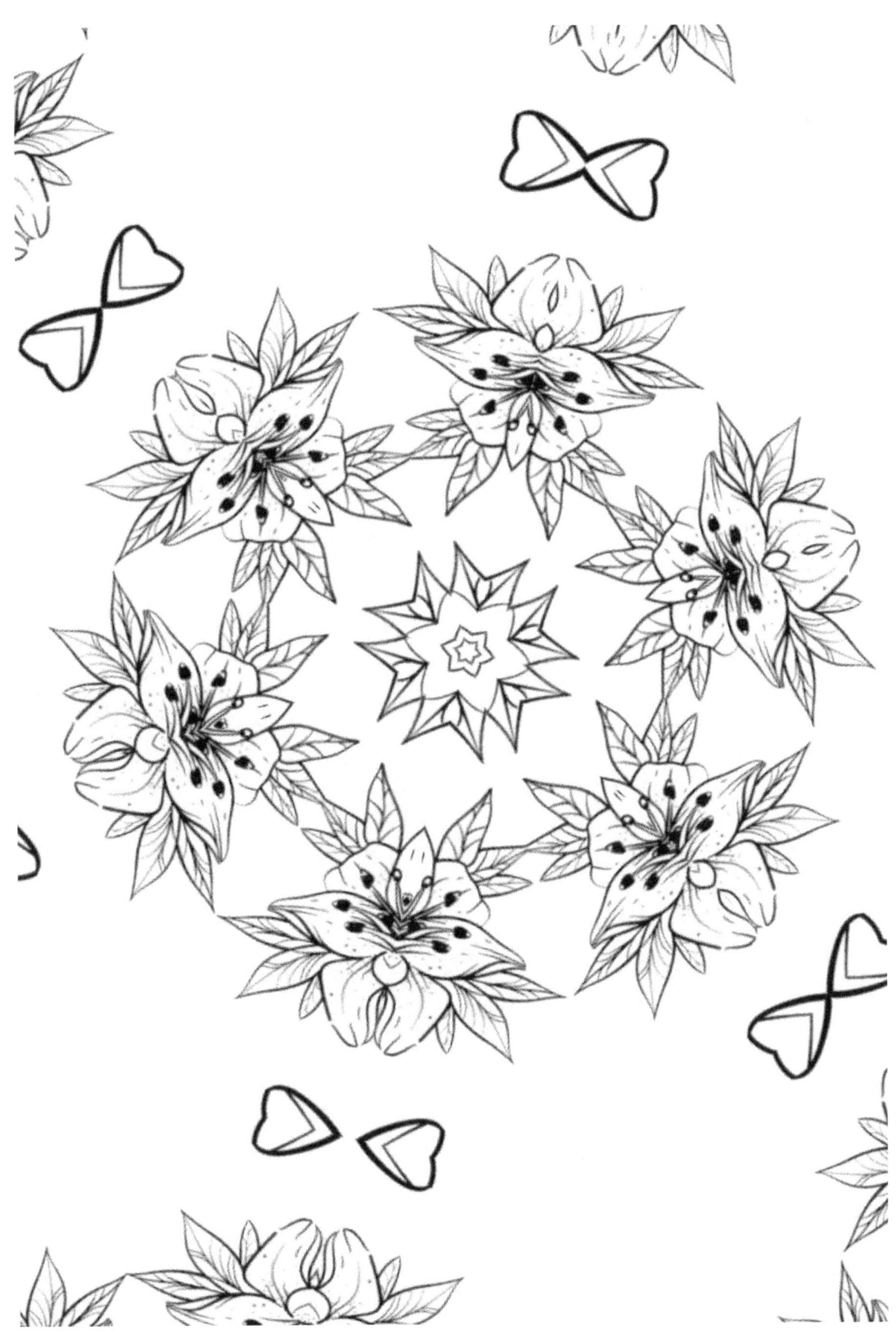

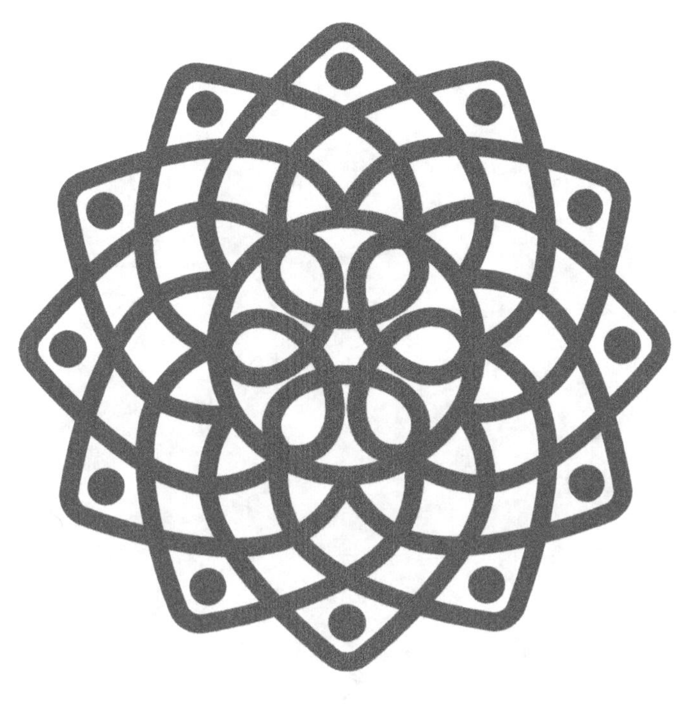

Check out our
other coloring
books here

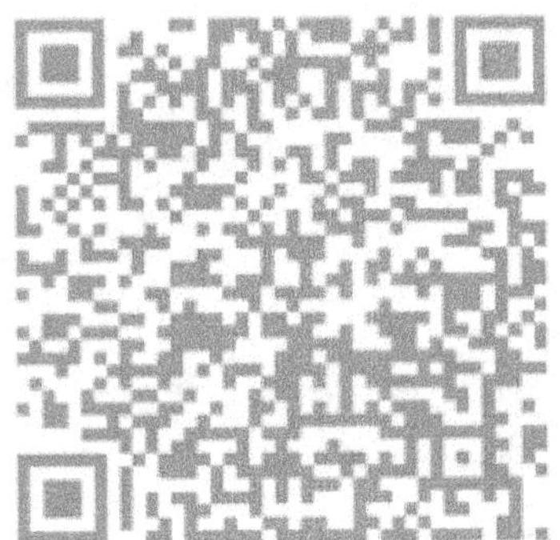